Praise for Joyful Creating

"Inspiring! A book to add to your library and reread again and again. Kate's fiery philosophy and joyful techniques are the antidote to burnout."

—Allison Vernon-Thompson,
Fitness Entrepreneur

"Joyful Creating is a breath of fresh air for anyone who has ever felt burnt out or disconnected from their spark. This is not just a guide to creativity; it's a reminder that joy is the fuel, not the byproduct, of meaningful work."

—Jill Lawrence,
Mindfulness and Meditation Teacher

"Joyful Creating is a love letter to your creative self. It's a gorgeous and uplifting journey into you and your process.

It has such lovely energy and I basked in it. It powered me up to create with renewed excitement!"

—Martha Dunlop,
Author, Starfolk Trilogy & Wild Shadow

"Joyful Creating reinforced the importance of creativity in my everyday life – not just as something to do but as a way of being. Life's so much richer now! I now look for the little sparks of magic in my daily life that fuel my bigger creative projects."

—Sheila LeClerc,
Executive and Leadership Coach

"Joyful Creating is the antidote to burnout culture, an empowering journey to reignite your creative mojo and learn to dance with your muse, rather than shoehorning your way through the artistic process."

—Michelle Reeves,
Author, The Happiness Habits Transformation

Joyful Creating

Stay Inspired Without
Losing Your Spark

KATE TREMILLS

Joyful Creating

© Kate Tremills 2025

Ebook Edition: October, 2025

ISBN: 978-1-987818-08-6

First Print Edition: October, 2025

ISBN: 978-1-987818-07-9

Book Cover by 100Covers

Published by RavenHeart Press

*For every creator discovering that joy
outranks hustle every time.*

Contents

Introduction

LITTLE MOMENTS OF JOY

SOME BOOKS COME IN a rush and others need grace and time. This book taught me to revel in the process.

Every creative endeavour has its own pace. Its own intention and purpose. Going against that ruins the essence of what you're birthing. And how you can grow.

I've created projects that came together in weeks — a fact that was a point of pride. Whether that's because I was rushed a lot as a child — or because we live in a world that values speed over experience — I thought that the faster a project happened, the better it was. Or to be clear, the better I was as a creative.

This, my loves, is the great lie.

Every project has its rhythm. Whether that takes a week or a year. It's easy to push our timeline on a project. But that rarely serves the outcome. This book wanted me to savour the journey. To remember what it feels like to experience the joy in every word.

Writing this came in little, intentional increments. I wrote this in small bursts, not big rushes of thousands of words. As I got deeper into the process, and grew to understand the rhythm, I saw why the pace needed to be slow.

Joyful Creating wanted me to walk my talk. To be in integrity with my desire for creatives. To live the experience of treasuring my time with the essence of this story.

This book wanted to be deeply and deliciously savoured. Not consumed. Not rushed. Not pushed and prodded. But lovingly, deeply crafted.

It's so easy for me to fall into a habit of pushing and prodding. To expect a project to follow my timeline and how I want it to happen. If I have learned anything as an artist and an entrepreneur, it's that the heart of a project has its own beat. Forcing it to be something it's not will only strip you of the joy you might feel.

When I pay close attention to the state of my creativity, I know what I need. Flow shuts off in a second when I stop breathing and start panicking. And opens up when I give myself room to trust and weave with the Divine.

Joyful Creating is a journey, a methodology, a commitment to the truest expression of your creative power. It's an approach that puts your wellbeing at the heart of your flow.

When you take back your creative rhythm, you discover your joy.

Healthy creative habits involve taking thoughtful care of your inspiration (inflow of energy) and conscious expression (outflow of energy). Rather than focusing obsessively on the production, I want you to give equal time to lighting your spark as you do blazing with it.

The secret to longevity is joy. Remembering what it felt like to create as a child. To chase an idea. To invent a world. To imagine grand inventions. To ride Saturn's rings.

Somewhere along the way, we got convinced that creativity is a means to accolades, riches, and adoring fans. And while that is occasionally true, it isn't the source of delight. Creative magic comes from awe. From wonder. And most of all, from listening to your heart.

When you stop listening to your heart, you give away your power.

Writing *Joyful Creating* is a long-time dream. An ode to my favourite people in the world - artists, makers, and entrepreneurs. The ones who dedicate their hearts to expressing their delight and enthusiasm in the world. This is my gift to you.

I've watched so many creatives, including me, burn themselves out to "make it" according to someone else's rules. Whether it was 18-hour days in the film industry, or 80-hour weeks in the startup world, or thinking I needed to be a novelist according to Amazon's rules and churn out 20 books a year.

In those times, I felt the joy of being creative wither and die.

The crushing effect of a high-output, fast-production approach leaves us tired and disheartened. After riding the roller coaster more times than I want to count, I realized that the creative journey is too magical to waste.

Joyful Creating is a call to reclaim your delight. To play in the fields of imagination. And rediscover the thrill of making. You choose how you want to contribute to this world. How you want to write your novel and build your business.

You are in charge of your experience. And you're essential to the creative culture that we make.

Together, we are a force to be reckoned with — a force for love, delight, silliness, and wonder.

May this book inspire you to feel the depths of your magic and the heights of your joy.

Chapter One

Joyful Creating

J OYFUL CREATING IS THE way to bring joy to whatever you make. Whether that's a book, business, community, podcasts, products, interior design, and more.

Being creative is the first thing I think about in the morning and the last thing on my mind at night. Assuming of course, that I'm not fretting about the world. But that's a topic for another day.

After taking my creativity for granted (more than once), I realized that being a healthy creative was a big source of my happiness in life. When I disrespected or ignored or shoved my creative inspiration away, I became bitter, resentful, and cynical. I deeply believe there is a thread between those states.

When I am expressed and courageous, I am confident and happy. When I push down my expression and put other things first for too long, I become grumbly and unhappy. We solve so much in our lives by expressing what's in our hearts. In seeing ourselves and giving our magic tangible form.

After years of writing and producing, I noticed that the world gives most of the attention to productivity. I love that. I live for that. And when I ran face-first into deep burnout (that shook my identity and my health), I was determined to find another way. To focus as much on tending my flame as burning with it.

At first, I conceived of this as one book. The first half about inspiration (creative inflow) and the second half about producing (creative outflow). As I was writing, I realized that these two parts needed their own books. Each was addressing a different desire and frustration.

This book focuses on restoring your creative energy — whether after completing a big project or a big day. The habits guide you to keep inspiration flowing and to stay in touch with your innate compass. The second book focuses on the habits that nurture joyful productivity without overwhelm (or perfectionism).

I imagine these books as sisters — each one supporting your creative flow.

This book is the antidote to burnout. Ditching the old messaging to learn a new way to feel great while you create and ride the storms that inevitably come when you are challenging yourself to learn something new.

My ideal world is filled with creative artists, makers, and entrepreneurs who live full lives and love what they do. Especially on the days when it frustrates the hell out of us!

Creating with joy is the way to connect to your intuition. To know that you're hearing your voice and following your path. It's trusting that you matter as much as anyone else. And that being vibrant and inspired is your ticket to creative flow.

My creative spark has been my greatest guide, my dearest friend, and my deepest source of delight. I want this for you. The second book shares all my sacred habits that build consistent momentum while staying connected to my muse. If this is the antidote to burnout, the second book is the remedy for overwhelm.

Use the inspiration and productivity habits for a moment, a day, a week, or a season. As you embrace them, you'll know when you need each one. If you build them into your rhythm, you'll feel how much they fuel you.

Joyful creating is:

~ An antidote to burnout culture.

~ A call to put your soul first.

~ A portal to the infinite imagination you had as a child.

~ A spark to the fire in your belly and the sunshine in

your heart.

~ A bolt of courage to catapult you into your dream.

You are designed to revel in your natural expression, your passionate heart, your calling to share a vision in paint, words, flowers, cupcakes, or computer code.

In each chapter, I share how to keep your creative heart (and mind) happy. When you tend to the creative inflow, the outflow becomes easier. When you tend to the outflow, you become confident and lighter of heart.

I hope you will avoid what I did for years - chasing other people's approval. I promise that it rarely delivers, and it never lasts. When you chase your own delight and joy? That is a recipe for contentment. And you'll have a song or book or podcast or quilt or phone app to show for it!

In essence, you are like a flower. You need sunshine, water, and healthy soil full of nutrients to flourish. Or, for creative folks, you need inspiration, creative stimulus, friendly conversations, innovative notions, and practice being in a receptive state. You need space and travel and people and books and movies and all kinds of inspiration.

It's like when I was first learning to ride a road bike and discovered, in a very humbling way, what the term *bonking* means. It's not the cheeky version! Basically, it means I rode WAY too far without fuelling my muscles. And once you reach that state on a ride? You're done. Your body has made its truth known. And it's time to hitch a lift and sleep it off until tomorrow.

The same can (and will) happen with your creative energy. You can push and push and push, but the tank will empty and you'll start spitting out fumes or repetitive, clichéd ideas. The joy of what you do will burn up and you'll get resentful, rather than innovative. I want your flowery self to be well-watered so that you make art and creations that fill you with pride.

Unhealthy work habits and burnout aside, focusing only on the outflow is missing a HUGE part of the joy of being creative. Half the journey is refilling your tank. Exploring the artistic offerings of other people. Discovering what lights you up and drives you to say something.

Taking time to be in the world, whether that's the forest or the city, is what fuels us as creators. After many years of trial and error, I learned that movement spurs the flow of creative imagination and inspiration. Some days, I need to go for a drive in my car. Others, I need the combination of music and dance. Or I feel the pull of a long walk.

I remind myself every day to check in with these tools. Not to expect that I will do them all! Instead, to ask myself, "What do I need today? What is the most important thing that I can give my creative heart on this gorgeous day? Is it rest? Is it play? Do I need fuel or do I need to flow?"

And like any great habit, it takes time to integrate them into your life.

The first and most important step to Joyful Creating is building trust in yourself. When you listen to your inner wisdom, you get clearer on what you need. And what you have to say. You know when you need to tend to yourself, and when you must shout your truth from the rooftops (or laptops).

Joyful Creating believes that *you* are the expert in being *you*. Your creativity is your closest ally, your dearest friend. And it will always be honest about what you need to feel the flow of your truth. As with any friend, the closer you listen, the better you hear.

And since so little space is given to tending your flame to keep it burning bright, this one is dedicated to nurturing *you* first. Then naturally progressing to the creative pull of your heart.

One last note...

In these pages, I may swear. I grew up in Nova Scotia, a land of fairies, pirates, and rogues with angelic voices. So it comes with the territory. I even played with the idea of calling this book *"Creative As Fuck"* (its official alternate title).

In the end, I chose to lead with the joy of it all.

I also use words like magic, divine, and ritual. I see creativity as a beautiful connection to the world, the universe, and my soul. If that's not your jam, I get it. But it is most definitely mine.

So if you love a good dose of fairy dust, mystical musings, and practical magic. You are in the right place.

Let's dive in!

Chapter Two

Joy Dates

WHEN I LEFT THE film industry to write novels, I made a vow. I swore to myself that I would get a life. I wanted to travel and have a garden and go for brunch with friends and learn skills that had absolutely nothing to do with my career.

To give a little bit of context, I had been working full time as a communications consultant while also building a career as a screenwriter and producer. The concept of *time off* or a *weekend* felt pretty damn foreign. I spent all my weekends researching and writing film and television scripts. Learning about storytelling. And networking to get my projects made.

Fast forward twelve years. Yes — twelve years of not really understanding what other folks considered fun. Or restorative. Or maybe even silly and entertaining.

When I finally made the leap, I panicked. What do I do when I'm not writing or networking or travelling? What do I focus on? What was this thing called *spare time*?

One day, I asked a friend in a whispered and slightly puzzled voice, "What exactly do people DO on their weekends?"

It would be easy to judge the former version of me. To wonder how she couldn't possibly understand the benefit of time off. Time to reflect and simply be herself. But I look back on that moment with so much love in my heart.

I adore that former version of myself. She was passionate and determined. Capable and committed. And she was about to make one of the greatest discoveries of her life.

Joy Dates.

These dates had one purpose. Whatever brought me joy.

It wasn't meant to further a project I was working on. Or improve me as a person. It wasn't research for a book. Or an activity that would impress anyone else.

Its sole and pure purpose was to bring me JOY.

You see, in the pursuit of work that I love, I thought I had to spend every waking moment pursuing it. But what that did was eventually drain me of curiosity and delight. It left me in a state of hustle and grind.

While some people aspire to be in that state constantly, I don't. And I really don't advise it for anyone else.

Periodically, yes! Absolutely. I choose to call it sprinting. When you need to push hard for a short and defined time in the service of a specific achievement.

Sprinting can work for completing a first draft of a screenplay. It also works for launching an online course or a book. It works when preparing for your first big film festival or gallery showing.

What it does not work for (a.k.a. hustle culture) is a constant approach to creating. We are human beings in decidedly human bodies that require movement, fresh air, real food, physical contact, and connection. I say this as someone who has run marathons (42km), biked Gran Fondos (160km plus mountains plus weather), and worked ridiculous hours during startup launches and the crazy-yet-amazing Toronto Film Festival.

When I weave joy into the regular fabric of my creative days, I am far more productive over the long-haul and I leave resentment in the dust. I'm also a LOT more fun to be around and a TON more aware of my emotional state — so that I don't dump it all over others.

Spending time away from my passionate work for the sake of lighting up my heart and igniting my curiosity puts me back in the purest state there is. *Childlike wonder.*

In that state, all your joy, delight, fascination and love get replenished. You rediscover who you are and what you care about. You reconnect to the world and its beauty.

You remember that there are many other people making wondrous and hilarious things.

I firmly believe that connecting with wonder and delight keeps me in touch with my truest essence and with the good in the world. As creatives, we're incredibly sensitive. We're designed to feel, connect, and receive. These precious abilities make it possible to create art, and products, and experiences that touch the hearts of other humans.

They also make us sensitive to the crushing reality this world serves up. The horrors and heartbreaks available to see anytime we open our phones or turn on our televisions. As early as elementary school, we're taught that numbing to these realities or pretending they don't affect us is *cool*.

Except cool doesn't make you a tender artist or a talented writer. Cool just makes you detached and distant. Being a creative that illuminates the world for others requires feeling and being open. Which, in my book (literally THIS book) comes from seeking and cultivating joy.

So. Step one in prepping for a Joy Date. Choose an activity or destination that has absolutely nothing to do with work or impressing others (Hello Instagram & TikTok!).

Step two is to commit to a date alone. No partners, friends, or children.

We'll talk later about Joy Date buddies and accountability partners. But when building a joy date practice, it's important to practice them alone.

Why? Because so many of us (especially women) will automatically want to take care of the other person. To ensure that they're getting their joy needs met. And in that process, we defer to another person's joy. Forgetting, or shoving aside, our own.

So. When experimenting with a joy date, do it solo. Consider this a beautiful (and possibly thrilling and uncomfortable) way to get to know YOU.

Being alone and leaning in to joy are the only two criteria of a joy date. While this sounds incredibly simple, it was amazingly hard for me at the start.

For one thing, while I had notions of what brought me joy, I rarely gave them much time. Let alone making a morning, afternoon, or whole day of it. That would send my Inner Taskmaster into a tizzy fit.

Yes, not just a tizzy or a fit. This was a tizzy fit. Much, *much* worse.

She was not at all convinced that these Joy Dates were productive. They sounded nice. Like something you reserve for the weekend and limit to an hour. But definitely not (as I am recommending) a date where you drive for as long as it takes to sit on a favourite beach and throw rocks in the water while being serenaded by ospreys.

Or take yourself to an art exhibit. Or ride your scooter onto a ferry then drive all around, grab a coffee, then scoot home. Or taking yourself out for a delectable dinner at your favourite restaurant with a book that you just cannot stop reading.

To my Inner Taskmaster, this all sounded like a terrible (and probably sinful) waste of time. For many of us, pleasure and joy have been deemed wasteful and immoral. When truthfully, they light us up and refill the creative idea banks.

So let's experiment! One practice that I talk about throughout this book is to attune to your body and intuition. They are your true north. Every time, they will guide you to what you need.

If you are exhausted and burnt out, your body is the canary in a coal mine. It will start with subtle signs, then move on to not-so-subtle signs that you need replenishment. Burnout can *definitely* turn into a physical issue like exhausted adrenal glands - like I had after years of emptying my energy tanks without taking the time to replenish them.

But if you train yourself to notice the subtle signs, to listen to your intuition, you can avoid the harsh signals. And trust me, you want to avoid the loud sirens of deep exhaustion. They take months and even years to heal.

This is why I want you to learn from my mistakes. My intuition (and body) had to scream at me and create some rather dramatic scenarios to get my attention. One of these was me committing to yet another Gran Fondo (160km) that included a 39km climb up Mount Baker in Washington state and an elevation climb of over 1400 metres. I had done this ride before so it didn't scare me. But this time, my body was exhausted. I had days when I pulled off a ride and others where I barely made it a few kilometres.

I was determined to overcome this challenge with willpower and determination. But trust me, when your body is as depleted as mine was by this point, you can throw all the affirmations and commitment in the world at it, and your body will win. I got part way into the ride, with every pedal stroke a laborious effort and my riding partner expressing utter frustration at me. When, part way up the mountain, the brakes on my bike SEIZED.

I have rarely been more grateful for the grace of the Universe than in that moment. I needed someone – ANYONE – else to tell me it was okay to stop. To let go. And if that came through the intelligence of my bike brakes? I would take it! I felt bad that I was letting down my riding partner, but I felt way more relieved to stop.

That experience is now etched in my mind. I remember every detail. Most of all, I recall being so deeply and profoundly relieved to be given a reason to stop. A reason that felt legitimate. I had not yet arrived at a place where I knew that my body's signals and my exhaustion were legitimate enough. Let alone being able to stand up for them when other people challenged me.

Every moment of this lesson can be applied to creative projects. There will be times when you are so wrung out that you need joy. You'll need joy and play like a car needs gasoline (or electricity). The big mindset and heartset shift that I want you to make is to know that joy is your fuel. As a creative, you need it. Regularly. Consistently.

When you neglect it, your engine will seize. Nothing will function correctly. And you'll find yourself stuck in the same place for days. Sharing the same stories. Writing the same boring sentences. Making the same marketing moves. Instead of being bold, imaginative, and alive.

***

What I aspire to as a commitment and habit (yes, I actually LOVE habits and rituals), is to book Joy Dates on a regular basis. To intentionally and proactively fuel my creative heart with the practice that the delightful Julia Cameron in The Artist's Way, calls an *artist date*:

"Artist Dates fire up the imagination. They spark whimsy. They encourage play. Since art is about the play of ideas, they feed our creative work by replenishing our inner well of images and inspiration."

I expanded the notion of an *artist date* to a *Joy Date*. Mostly because I found my brain wanting to limit my options to artistic (or what I perceived as artistic) events. And I would instinctively shut down the practice because the ideas didn't feel joyful to me.

In asking myself if I have been on a Joy Date this week, I can honestly answer. And because my brain defaults to asking my heart whether I have produced enough this week rather than have I felt enough joy, I need these not-so-subtle reminders.

I often feel like I am re-patterning centuries of cultural training toward production and proving my worth, to re-orient towards joy.

I still ask, how could joy possibly open space for more inspiration? Except, it *does*.

Take this moment. And let the word *joy* resonate in your heart.

Can you feel it open the channels in your body?
Do you sense your inner five-year-old breaking free from her little box to grab the reins?
Do you breathe a little deeper and find a tiny smile dancing

on your lips?

Is it light and playful, energetic and even silly?

I believe that joy is a portal. A doorway into fantastical realms. Whether those realms contain mystical, magical stories or the answer to a mathematical theorem. Joy feels and looks different to each of us and still... it is the portal to effortless inspiration.

The other element that I love that Julia Cameron points out is the "solo" expedition.

Joy dates are meant to be for you. Savouring your own space. Booking these dates is a beautiful gesture to honour creativity. Giving back all it has given you. Another reason the solo adventure matters is that you'll have a more intimate dialogue with the Divine.

Being with people is a distraction. A wonderful, sometimes inspiring distraction. But it also pulls my attention away from the experience of dancing with divinity. When I am alone, I soak in every sensual detail. I notice features that would blur by if I were in conversation. I take time to relax and be with the ideas or "drop-ins" that come to me.

Anyone who has danced with a particularly inspired or tenuous idea knows that, at first, it's a little like catching a glimpse of a fairy. It takes you off guard, sparkles in your heart, and can be fleeting if you don't stop and take in the offering.

Being alone with creative inspiration is a practiced art. One full of nuance and patient attention. It also means knowing yourself well enough to understand if you are purely taking in sensory delights or if you are meant to be catching fairy dust.

I'm not sure why Julia Cameron suggests taking these dates weekly, but for me, it's as much to understand my own season as it is to fill my creative well. When I go out on a joy date, I get a sense of whether I am tired, inspired, bored, ready to chase a new idea, dangerously close to abandoning one project for something shinier, or just in need of a week-long rest.

I wouldn't lean into the subtleties of my energetic state if I am on an outing with others. I am distracted by their energetic and emotional state, and the dialogue that is usually expected when with others. Joy Dates are intentionally for YOU.

Instead of tending to others, I am drinking in the full thrill of perceiving the world.

***

How do you know which Joy Date suits you? You start!

Truly. You may not know right away. And you'll probably have to build the habit a few times before you get a sense of what works for you and what doesn't.

Think of your journey with Joy Dates much like your journey with a creative endeavour, skill, or a new risk that you're taking. The thrill is in the discovery. And the nourishment is in committing the time. Even if the actual activity doesn't quite land for you, knowing that you took the time to try makes ALL the difference.

The other blessing that comes with Joy Dates is you get to know yourself. You find out what may work for others that doesn't work for you. And vice versa.

Some folks might love those wine and paint nights. I've tried one. It was not very fun for me. Meanwhile, I have resisted doing vision boards forever. Rolled my eyes whenever they came up. And when I attended an all-day make your board workshop, I had the *best* time.

I still think about that day when I look at my board that I created. I adore the board so much, I have it in my creative office. Joy Dates are meant to surprise you. Break you out of your comfort zone. Get you to think about activities or places that bring fresh energy.

If you're like me, you adore a list of ideas to get you started. Half the reason I love a good list is so I can knock off the stuff that I don't like! To sort through the ideas and find the one that sparks a nervous feeling in my tummy and anticipation in my heart.

I'd love to get you started with your Joy Date list:

Nature

~ Drive to a beach

~ Hang out in a grove of trees

~ Listen for all the birds where you live

~ Go stargazing

~ Jump on the train and get off at a spontaneous stop

~ Go to a neighbourhood you've never explored

Artistic

~ Grab a sketchbook and a pencil

~ Buy and use a colouring book

~ Build a playlist

~ Journal an interaction with a lovely famous person

~ Bake and decorate a gluten-free cake

~ Try on bold outfits at a store

Foodies

~ Find a new cafe

~ Take a cooking class

~ Learn mixology
~ Take a novel out for dinner (and read it)
~ Stay overnight in a fancy hotel

Playful

~ Dance inside or outside or under the moon
~ Skip your way down thirty blocks in the city
~ Play Jenga by yourself
~ Sing at karaoke
~ Take yourself glamping (glamorous camping)

The thrill of committing to Joy Dates is that they build their own momentum. If you're still feeling resistant, start by creating your own list. Grab one or two ideas from above and dare yourself to write in a journal for at least ten minutes.

I promise that once you get going, you'll have fun coming up with random and wild ideas.

Writing that list transported me back to waking up as a little girl. And how every day was this wide-open slate of coming up with things to do. Back before to-do lists and obligations. When the notion of getting to make up what you were going to do and who you were going to be was a thrilling adventure. When you still believed in possibilities and daring chances.

That is the point of Joy Dates.

Reconnecting to that wild abandon and wonder in your heart. They don't need any purpose other than tethering you to pure vitality. Waking up that inner rebel, the wild goof, the delightful temptress, and any other gorgeous archetype you want to embody.

***

Let's talk about what might cause resistance to unwavering Joy Dates.

If you are a woman, you may baulk at the idea of joy dates weekly. I do, and I have been doing it for years. I do, and I don't have children (only a dog and kitty). I do, and I am practised at respecting my creative needs. I do, and I am shocked that *every single time*, I battle the guilt demon to take time for myself (that doesn't involve an errand).

I wish I could promise that this practice will be easy. I really can't promise that. This is a choice that needs to be utterly, purely for *you*. It will feel selfish. It will push your buttons. It will sound frivolous to others. And they may project their judgement at you.

If you grew up in a family that prized hard work over everything and instilled that you earn your worth by doing, doing, doing, or hustling your butt off, it will push multiple buttons. And if you grew up in North America, you're guaranteed to have some of that programming even if your family did not instil it.

How does this resistance show up? For me, it appears as a harsh little voice in my head. It will change the theme of the message depending on what might push my buttons.

We all have one of these. Rachel Hollis (author of *Girl, Wash Your Face* and *Girl, Stop Apologizing*) calls hers, Pam. Whether this is someone else's critical voice or our internalized shame, the real power is in airing these thoughts out into the sunshine. Like airing out a musty closet, they'll lose all their potency ... and fade away.

I'll share a few of the (highly shame-based) thoughts that show up for me. Imagine reading these in a snarky, harsh, mean-girl voice.

How old are you? Ten? Go back to work.
What grown adult leaves her desk and wanders around on a work day.
Really? You think joy is the magic solution to getting your work done?
Everyone else is moving so much faster than you. I wonder why. This is ridiculous. You are ridiculous. No wonder you'll never succeed.

Yeah. THAT'S resistance at her finest. Except the thing about resistance is the louder she yells, the more it's a sign that the project you are working on is important. The more resistance you feel to Joy Dates, the more they will deliver your creative juice.

You might discover that going on a Joy Date is the activity that frees you from being stuck. Or it delivers the answer to a plot problem that you've been struggling to find. Or suddenly you download (intuitively receive) all the lessons in the course you want to make.

Of all the things I do to nurture creativity, Joy Dates are by far the ones that I resist the most. My guess is that it's because I can't accomplish it in 15 minutes! Joy Dates require time and intention. They give back what you put into them.

When I can't convince my mind to get on board with a Joy Date, the mindset trick that I use is to change its name. My delightful alternative name is *Romancing your Muse*.

Somehow, the beautiful notion of giving back to my muse works like magic. I've mysteriously forgotten about her until I invoke her name. The moment I do, I feel how beautiful it is to be a creative being. My muse reminds me that a key to being creative is also being in the world.

Did we really think chaining ourselves to a desk was the only way to receive inspiration? Who came up with that notion, anyway?

Romancing your Muse is all about taking her out to see the autumn leaves. Or visiting that sweet shop that's full of magical jewellery. It's singing to her as you drive. Or taking the subway to the best teahouse you've been stalking on Instagram.

And if you're someone (like me) who struggles to come up with ideas, keep a Joy Date notebook. I love the little pocketbooks by Rifle Paper Co. or a sweet company close to me called Linden Paper Co. I will collect ideas as they come to me. Sometimes, they have a particular date.

One of my favourite activities is going to craft shows. I get to ogle beautiful artistic items, chat with other makers, drink coffee while I peruse, and soak in all the colour, scents, and buzz. It's absolute heaven. Unless it's in too small a space and way too crowded. I love a little elbow room! Especially when browsing.

Whatever gives my Muse joy, gives me joy. And however the tricky mindset shift works, I'll take it! Romancing your muse is part of the creative maker job description. Gathering ideas, sparking inspiration, tending to your imaginative heart ~ it's a time-honoured, essential way of being.

We need to fuel both our sensual hearts and our action-craving souls. Our feminine and masculine sides are equally important to being joyful and productive creatives. If you lean more heavily to the feminine – of receiving, then be sure to tend to your masculine of producing. If you lean more towards your masculine of acting, be sure to love up your feminine of dreaming.

My guess is that I'll need to keep a sharp eye on my tendency to work harder than necessary for the rest of my days. So if you find this sneaky little belief showing up regularly, know that you are in great company! We get to challenge that core belief together. Along with every other woman in the world. Imagine the tidal shift we are creating!

What I can promise you is that every time, you will feel grateful. Every time, you will feel your shoulders relax and your solar plexus expand. Every time, you will find the joyful crinkle around your eyes and the softness in your heart. Every time, you'll be gifted with a tender discovery of what truly matters to you.

***

And I love offering tips to make this practice easy to adopt and fun to maintain.

If a date is important to me, it goes in my calendar. Whether I'm picking up my puppy or meeting a creative partner for coffee, I book it. Treating Joy Dates like a commitment that matters means putting it in my calendar. It's a heck of a lot harder to forget or blow it off when the reminder pops up.

Another approach is to have a Joy Date partner. Make it a challenge that you can share. You won't be going on the dates together. Instead, they're your celebration partner and cheerleader. Having someone you're accountable to and who will cheer for you when you accomplish your date, makes such a difference. And the more you do it, the better it feels!

You can also share what you did on your date! You'll be amazed how sharing about your adventures makes them feel richer and will inspire your friend on her dates. The magic of sharing really gives habits momentum. Plus, the promise of delivering to your friend is another way to trick your Inner Taskmaster into going on the date instead of punking out.

Keeping my commitments to my friends is important. Especially when I know that my leap will inspire (and challenge) her to take *her* leap. Like a sublime relay race. We pull one another toward our joy and powerful creating. While we break down centuries of patriarchal competition in one consistent act.

If one of your challenges is feeling like you've lost touch with joy or play, the beauty of these dates is that they reconnect you with those qualities. They are inside you.

People may have ignored or neglected them for so long that you need to coax them out of hiding. Tend to them like a delicate flower that needs to be watered and watched to spring back to life.

Even if you are coming out of a drought season or a time or immense challenge, those qualities never go away. They are an intrinsic part of your creative nature. They may have been shoved and mocked and even shamed for years.

If that's the case, you'll feel especially challenged and triggered by my suggestion of a weekly Joy Date. And it's even more essential for those of us who believe that these dates are frivolous, irrelevant, wasteful, or downright irritating.

The more we push away our joy and wonder, the more brittle and jaded our creativity becomes. Until it decides to pack its bags, cross its arms, and wait sullenly in a corner until you come to your openhearted senses.

I promise that I'm not speaking hypothetically. I've gone through some particularly harsh seasons of wondering whether I might ever experience the delight of creative excitement again.

Here are a handful of my own creative drought seasons:

- After I left the film industry in a rather spectacular fashion, rejecting a film deal that everyone (except my agent) assumed was a done deal.

- After I burnt out my adrenal glands and could not feel motivation, let alone enthusiasm, and was convinced that I would never feel joyful and creative again.

- After a deeply challenging season in my marriage, that led to moving to a new home - and distancing me from almost every friend I had.

Each of those seasons was followed by a creative drought that scared me. I wasn't sure who I was anymore and whether I was going to find my creative heart again. I now believe that had I insisted on doing Joy Dates through those dry spells, I would have kept one hand on my inner compass. And might have passed through the desert faster.

At the very least, I would have been tending to my heart and taking care of myself. Both need to be priorities for a creative. Because you are inherently a joyful being full of ideas and inspiration.

When seasons come along that wipe your joy away, you have a clear indication that you need to tend to yourself. To get support. To ask what you need.

These tools have delightful names because I believe that being a creative human is a precious gift. And still, they require the heart of a lioness. To believe that you deserve the time. To insist on taking care of yourself, especially in the hard times.

Joy Dates are like good sleep, whole food, kind friends, and a soft pillow. Essentials for you to be in touch with yourself and your voice.

Making regular time for Joy Dates preps your system to receive ideas. Being creative is a dance between receiving inspiration and transforming that into your offering. The time that you give to Joy Dates comes back to you tenfold in the ideas that you receive. It also cultivates the practice of remembering that you live in a generous universe. One that wants to spark your ideas.

When you go on a Joy Date, you're remembering what it feels like to receive.

Chapter Three

Receiving

C ULTIVATING JOY IS ESSENTIAL to being connected to wonder. To remembering that you're a star in a vast universe. There is a way to feel supported in your expression.

Being healthy and vibrant as a creative means *receiving* the flow of ideas. To trust, with a curious heart, that you're being guided. That you're not all alone on the journey.

So before I dive into inspiration, let's have a little chat about receiving.

We're in the middle of a great cultural shift. You and I are part of it. The fact that you hold this book in your hands is proof.

Proof that you want a different way. Proof that you believe in the magic of creating. Proof that you're doing this in partnership (with support). And it can be soooo much easier than it's been before (or than you were raised to believe).

The pervasive global culture is one of pushing, forcing, and focusing on the bottom line. We have absorbed the Western industrial view of life. It's controlled our perception of work, value, productivity, and importance.

As more people (especially women) reject burnout culture, we're discovering that so many other aspects have value. Our wellbeing, joy, connections, community, ecosystems, creativity, spirituality, and more.

These are traditionally associated with the feminine (independent of gender). While many cultures put this first, they've been overshadowed and bullied by the pursuit of profit. The pursuit of fame. The need to conquer and win at all costs.

I share this as someone who loves to win — against my own limiting beliefs. I have a feisty, fiery moon sign that thrives on challenges. My satisfaction often comes from conquering obstacles and inner fears. So for the longest time as a young woman, I conflated my need to break through old limitations with winning over others. After all, that's what the culture wanted me to believe was the path to feeling good and accomplished.

Oh boy, was that wrong. The closer I got to success in the film industry, the clearer it became what I was giving up. And it was feeling a lot like the messaging people repeated about success. Especially — "It's lonely at the top."

I saw what I was sacrificing — not only my health (my poor adrenal glands were SO over my long hours) but also my relationships. My circle of friends was wonderful, but limited to people only in the film biz who understood the crazy hours. And while I am sure they would have been happy for me to get a deal, it was feeling lonelier and lonelier.

That didn't feel one iota like success to me. My vision of success was having a core group of wonderful friends who would clink glasses of champagne (preferably in Rome or Paris) and cheer each other's brilliance. Who knew we were building something together — for ourselves and the world.

I realized that I needed to do things differently. And that decision changed everything. I didn't know it right away — but I began decluttering messaging that had influenced me for decades.

I was seeking a new way. *A joyful way.*

A way that involved trust and faith and listening closely to the guidance of the Universe. Even when I felt like I was groping in the dark to find the way out of the tunnel. And the beautiful gift available by opting into this path — this practice of receiving guidance — is that it's the antidote to burnout. It is the secret to rediscovering vitality. And being in creative flow.

As we weave the feminine back into our collective culture and show that we value it by making receiving a priority, the world is shifting. Our communities are shifting. Our lives are shifting.

And in this shift, we are reclaiming the creative dance. The art of trusting. Remembering that humans are not the centre of everything. We are only one element in the universal dance of life. The thrill in this shift is that the more we remember to receive, the easier and more delightful it is to create!

Maybe like me, you were raised to believe the whole thing is a solo adventure. Only you at the helm, forging forward with your novel, company, or big project. When you let that idea go, the process becomes a sacred partnership with the infinite brilliance of the divine. And let me tell ya, the universe is FULL of amazing ideas!

Building receptivity back into your life feels a little counter-intuitive. Or even counter-cultural. At first, it will feel awkward.

Like you're relearning a skill that is rusty or got pushed into a faint memory. It may feel like you're doing it all wrong. Or like you're cheating. Because when you trust your creative vision — really trust it — the energy flows through you with impressive power.

When you receive your vision, you'll write, paint, design, speak so much faster. For me, the indicator that

I was on the right creative wave was the feeling of bliss. The smile that appears on my face. And the pure relief of trusting myself.

There is one prerequisite to being ready to receive a creative vision and pour it into a project, is that you need to know your craft. It's important to have a solid and dependable container to catch the creative vision. If you're new to a medium, the most important step is to learn from the people you admire. The brilliance of this is that it's just a different form of receiving!

In my case, it meant understanding the mechanics (and art) of what made a great story. The structure, genre expectations, and the emotional impact. In your case, it might be what makes a powerful song or how to be a compelling podcast host. I dive deeper into the power of Study in a later chapter.

And each of these is simply a different stage of learning and receiving with grace. The people who came ahead of you are giving you the gift of observing what you like and what you don't. They're saving you the time you might have put into trying certain techniques or technology.

Once you have that inner scaffolding, you are ready to receive creative insight and inspiration with gusto! Bringing conscious awareness to it will completely change your creative game.

When I was on the cusp of leaving the film biz, I wrote my most powerful and impactful screenplay. This script got me meetings all over town and still gets interest from directors. Not only was it my best writing, I wrote it twice as fast as any other script to that date.

What was the difference? Why was this script special? What happened to set it apart?

After I had done the research and roughly outlined my story, I made a significant change to my writing process. I sourced exactly the right music to listen to while I was writing the scenes. Music that set the mood for the action and tension I wanted to convey.

Then, I created my first ritual of calling in my guides and the muse. I calmed my body and made the decision that this story would come through me. I didn't need to overthink it. I'd done my preparatory work.

The story was ready to be birthed. My job was to show up and be the conduit for grace.

In other words, I made a choice. Instead of pushing the story forward, I decided to follow it. To collaborate with the divine muse and trust the hands of inspiration. I convinced my over-active, controlling mind so the characters could lead the way.

This choice changed my creative process and products forever.

I used to think, forge, outline, think again, edit, and rework. You can feel the effort in those words, can't you? I certainly can. And that's what I had been told. Over and over. Keep "efforting."

Every practice includes its lessons. In my early days of writing, creating, and collaborating, I was a master of getting things done. Diving into learning. Pushing things forward. Getting together with others. And writing dozens of movie scripts.

Pushing, doing, making, and being in constant action was my permanent setting. I had absolutely no idea (yet) about the power of receiving. I'm sure that I was collaborating with the divine muse. I just had a habit that was deeply reinforced by my industries, of pushing, hustling, trying, executing, and rarely truly listening.

I believe and feel that my research, brainstorming, and outlining made that magical creation experience possible. They forged, as I like to call it, the scaffolding for the creation. I felt confident to fall back into the arms of inspiration because I had done that initial planning.

That's when the shift happened. I made a trust fall. You know that move where you allow yourself to fall back into the arms of someone, trusting that they will catch you? I'm not sure that I've ever successfully done that with a human being. But in this case, I did it with the muse.

I trusted that the story knew exactly where to take me. The agreement between me and these characters was forged in the research and outlining stage. Now, my job was to show up at the keyboard and capture magic.

Not only did I write that screenplay much faster, but it had a power to it. It's like anyone reading it felt the intensity that made it happen. Then the interest and the meetings started rolling in. And I had to confront a LOT of old beliefs about how "hard" the creative process needed to be.

Now, I'd been writing since I was a teenager and writing screenplays for over nine years. So it's not to say that becoming a seasoned writer or creative doesn't take time. Mostly, I believe it takes time to hone your craft and get to know who you are as a person and an artist.

But the actual process? We have so many stories and books and talks that go on about how hard it is to be creative. When I suspect that the hard part is really, as Steven Pressfield (author of *The War of Art* and *Going Pro*) calls it, "Resistance."

He shares this in *The War of Art*:

"Resistance has no strength of its own. Every ounce of juice it possesses comes from us. We feed it with power by our fear of it. Master that fear and we conquer Resistance."

While you might be tempted to think that Resistance is a necessary part of the process, I disagree. Resistance is a melange of all the ideas we ever soaked up from our parents, hometown, culture, television, media, friends, neighbours, and any other influence that told us some "truth" about our value, purpose, meaning, and most definitely, what it is to be creative.

In other words, Resistance is the hard part. Making a commitment to your dream and sticking to it is the hard part. Choosing what really matters to your heart and showing up for it is the hard part. It's hard because it requires courage and determination. Two qualities that have incredible value.

And once you show up? Once you sit down and write? Or go to the Improv class? That's when the magic happens. That's when grace and inspiration arrive. And if you trust it, if you make yourself *receptive* to your creative brilliance, you'll feel the flow.

Just like showing up, trust is a practice. I didn't write that screenplay and suddenly have words flowing out of me like Mozart channelling a symphony. Nope. Every time I sat down to write, I said a prayer. A prayer for trust and grace. For me to relax into collaboration with the divine muse.

I said this prayer in acknowledgment of the power flowing through me. That I am the conduit and the craftsperson who is collaborating with the mystery of creation. Which, to be honest, makes the whole adventure a lot more fun!

That prayer — my ritual of receiving — made all the difference when I shifted from writing scripts to writing novels. I knew a LOT about story structure, characters, and the discipline of writing. And I knew very little about writing a novel.

That did not stop the divine muse from delivering the story that became my first novel. In fact, it showed up (and kept showing up) while I was still in the film biz and had absolutely no interest in writing a fantasy tale. The more I pushed it aside, the stronger the character's insistence became. So strong, that I had begun a totally different novel until this one threw a fit.

At that point, I realized that this incredible story had chosen me. Not only that, but I was ready to receive it. The smartest choice to make was to clear the decks and write. And much like that amazing screenplay, this book had a life of its own. The more available and trusting I was, the faster the story flowed.

Until months later, I had my first novel. And I was hooked.

I had no interest in going back to push, push, shove, shove, try, try. I wanted to keep creating in harmony with the stories that showed up to be delivered and to change me. When a story showed up that intrigued me enough to go the distance, I knew it was a sacred pairing. That the two of us — the tale and me — had chosen each other like any divine partnership.

If I don't have enough curiosity about an endeavour, I won't put in the work that's required. This is an essential truth to learn about yourself. Starting creative projects is *much* easier for me than getting them across the finish line. Some people are the opposite. It takes a Herculean effort to get started, but once they're going, they're committed.

Not me. I have to be choosy up front. Consulting my creative intuition and being boldly honest about whether I am going to be there for this project. All the way. Not just halfway. Because when I do that? I slowly, persistently chip away at my creative confidence.

***

Even with those magical and life-changing experiences, I knew that I was a rookie at receiving. I had a lot to learn and even more to unlearn.

When you grow up believing that you need to constantly prove your value, trusting that it's safe to receive is tricky. Everything in me has been wired to anticipate, act, change, engage. Being in motion feels wired to my survival.

Combine that with two powerful mythologies ~ an artist myth that you need to build your work alone and an entrepreneur myth that's all about action and hustle? Well, you end up with the car gear always stuck in drive.

One of the hardest and best things to happen to me was the exhaustion of my adrenal glands. I burnt out on a deep physical level. This sounds innocent, but it rocked my world.

I was used to juggling two careers, a busy physical activity schedule (that included marathons and gran fondos), and fitting my tiny social and spiritual life in the cracks. My socializing happened with people who shared my creative passions, consulting industry, or physical activity.

While it was great to be surrounded by people who are passionate and physically fit, I was locked in a rhythm of pushing hard and never stopping to recognize that there just might, possibly, be an easier way of living my life. Let alone enjoying my creativity.

And so, as life tends to do, I got served a HUGE lesson. One that physically forced me to pause, let go, tend to my body. The shift was incredibly uncomfortable. For the first time in years, I had to rest and feel. It was like all the emotions of over a decade came rushing in.

Basically, after years of pushing hard, I burnt out HARD. I'd experienced small waves of exhaustion ~ after big projects or scary leaps ~ like covering the Toronto Film Festival and figuring it out on the fly. When the big burnout hit, each time I thought I could go back to my busy habits, my body would remind me that I had no gas in the tank.

For a year, I would rest a little then try to get back on the busy horse. It would work for a week, then I'd get hit by another wave of exhaustion. Each time, the wave got stronger and lasted longer. Until I sought help from my naturopath. He confirmed that I was in adrenal exhaustion. And if I insisted on my old habits, I would push those lovely glands to a point of no return.

That's how people end up with chronic fatigue syndrome. His warning worked. I took his guidance seriously — which was an overhaul of how I run my life. Ditching the juggling act of always being on the go. And learned to sit with the discomfort of my many emotions that had been waiting years for me to feel them.

I began the long road to listening to my body and my emotions. I also surrounded myself with people who prioritized well-being over proving themselves. It took a while to change the patterns I'd built my life around. But every step was worth the long-term change.

A few years later, I moved out of the big city to a beautiful property on Vancouver Island. Eventually, finding a lovely community of healthy entrepreneurs and artists. I learned to listen to my inner voice first ~ a choice that pays off in my happiness and authentic relationships.

The change wasn't easy because I'd pushed it away for a long time. So if my experience can spare you from going down the same road? I will be doubly grateful.

***

Taking care of your wellbeing while you create your dream projects is a better way to build a creative life. It's designed for longevity and for trusting that the divine muse wants to collaborate with you every step of the way. Why would you ever want to do something alone when you could ride a wave of love, support, and magic?

When life stopped me in my overachieving, burnout tracks, I created a committed meditation practice. I swiftly realized that the stronger my ability to meditate got, the better I became at listening and receiving. I got more comfortable with silence. And with hearing the wisdom being offered to me from the Universe.

I noticed more details. More messages. I heightened my awareness of my responses and the responses of others. I took in life on a deeper level. I reconnected with the subtle energies of nature and physical spaces. I realized that there were layers to this experience that I had rushed past in my hurry to accomplish and finish.

I realize that I'd been supported the whole way. I just hadn't been listening. And I definitely wasn't comfortable receiving. It felt like cheating. Like getting a hand somehow showed that I wasn't strong enough or capable enough to do it on my own.

That, my dear friends, is a bald-faced lie. A lie that I got sold through my cultural upbringing, schooling, and corporate experience.

We are designed to collaborate. To receive brilliant support from others in their genius zone. While we offer them the support of our genius zone. If you haven't heard this phrase "genius zone," I discovered it through the beautiful work of Gay Hendricks in his book, *The Big Leap*.

It's the feeling of being in complete alignment with the creative flow. Where time disappears. Ego no longer matters. And you are in harmony with joy. The more you're able to lean into your zone of genius, the more you experience expansion.

In the words of Gay Hendricks, "Your capacity expands in small increments each time you consciously let yourself enjoy the money you have, the love you feel, and the creativity you are expressing in the world. As that capacity for enjoyment expands, so does your financial abundance, the love you feel, and the creativity you express."

Receiving is a muscle. Much like focus. Commitment. And believing in yourself. Receiving takes practice. Especially if, like me, you are an Olympic athlete in the sport of doing. I had to learn to receive in little increments. Like a child learning to walk. I started with receiving compliments with grace.

Before you dismiss that idea, ask yourself, "Do I receive compliments and kudos with grace? Or do I swat them away like unwanted mosquitoes that make me cringe?"

I find that the real power of receiving is about the smaller moments rather than big gifts or accomplishments. The little gestures from strangers, like a smile or a kind word or admiring your hair. The offer of a seat on the subway or easy merging onto the highway.

The moments that we often brush away to move on with our lives. To get to the next destination. I lived my career that way for over a decade. Only to wonder what happened to my thirties?

When I notice the small interactions, I have much more depth and availability to receive the bigger ones. Without practising receiving, you may very well arrive at a big deal (like winning an Oscar or having a bestselling book or getting your dream job) with no capacity to let it in.

I fully admit that receiving has been an incredibly uncomfortable practice. It means feeling like I am being seen. That someone is noticing. That I've been thrown under a spotlight. When really, it is a moment of connection.

I want you to practise this with me. I want a world filled with creatives who are ready and willing to connect. That want to see and be seen. The more I expand my ability to receive, the more I receive from the world around me. The colours, the light, the joy, the seasons, the emotions. These are an intricate and delightful part of being in this life and on this planet.

Even if the thought of receiving from humans makes you cringe with awkwardness, there is a whole world of receiving from animals, nature, stories, travel, and a long list of possibilities. The more you notice, the more you will notice. The more you feel held and understood. The more connected you feel to your creations and the world they're destined to be in.

Receiving expands your capacity to collaborate, connect, and create. It's the essential switch from your creative output to creative input. To acknowledge that the flow goes both ways. That by receiving you are nurturing yourself and filling your cup. A magically different experience than constantly draining your energy, pushing beyond your limits, and believing you have to grind yourself into dust to accomplish your dreams.

It's the secret key to sustaining a long and happy creative life.

Without receiving, you will inevitably get burnt out, tired, resentful, or jaded. All states that will constrict your creative energy and eventually lead you to the experience of feeling blocked. Which, in my experience, is an invitation to ask what you've been doing that isn't working for you or your joy. An invitation to change and to show up for yourself in a new way.

When I feel cranky, resentful, jealous, or downright fed up with the world, I look for an opportunity to receive. Whether it's sunlight, a sweet scene in a book, a kind gesture from my puppy, or a moment of understanding from a friend, it melts the hard ice of bracing against the world. And opens me to a glimmer of connection.

A remembering that I am a part of an intricate and beautiful dance that forges this universe each day. In that remembering, I reconnect with my heart and my desire to contribute — essential components in my joy of being alive.

*****

Much like Joy Dates, the best approach to receiving is to make it an aware and consistent practice.

I started with welcoming small gifts. Receiving a smile from a kind barista. Letting in a friend's compliment when she loved my earrings. Taking a moment to feel the love in a hug being offered. Receiving the sweet grace of deliciousness and caffeine in my morning cappuccino. Taking in the wisdom from pulling my morning tarot cards.

Conscious receiving takes me out of my head and into my heart. It reminds me that I have this treasure of a body. And puts me into the present. Instead of hanging out in the future or in the past. Which tends to be where my mind goes most of the time.

One of the tricky things about being a creative is that I spend a LOT of time up in my head. Imagining, dreaming, strategizing, and editing. Those are such beautiful talents, *and* it takes intentional practice to spend time that isn't up in my head.

I remind myself regularly to come back into my heart, into my body. To engage with my receptive power. To remember that being in my body allows the flow to happen faster and easier. I can get caught in overthinking whirlpools if I don't remember to breathe and drop into my body. Journalling, meditation, dance, and spending time in nature are all key tools in my receptive toolkit.

I start my day by taking my puppy outside. In the summer, I breathe in the sparkling sunlight. In the winter, I stare at the stars and bask in the moonlight. The fresh air sweeps away my dreams and calms my already busy mind.

After that, I meditate to give myself "roots" for the day. When I skip meditating, I am easily blown this way and that by my thoughts. I've discovered that I need to be grounded in my breath and body to proceed intentionally. If my mind is still chewing on a problem or frustration, I pull out my journal. I pour all those thoughts and feelings into my journal. A practice that always lifts the mental clouds and brings the bright rays of insight.

The other grounding practice I use is pulling tarot cards for the energy of the day. It reminds me that each day has its own lessons. Every moment brings challenges and gifts. The tangible act of closing my eyes, shuffling the cards, breathing into my heart, asking an intentional question, then pulling the cards — gives me both a connection to the Divine and to my creative path.

The more intentional I am, the deeper the receptivity. When I shuffle the cards, I notice the energy. When I pull the cards, I read the message. When I look closer at the cards, I take in the beauty of the art and the insights in the symbols. I might open a tarot book and receive even more wisdom from my favourite tarot author.

I'm filled with gratitude ~ for the magic swirling around me, the writer who made the messages, the artist who painted the cards, and the teachers who guided me along the way. And for my spirit being open to the subtle gifts of elements and archetypes.

I encourage you to practice every day — with little moments and bigger opportunities. As you build your practice, you'll notice the little wins, and create capacity for the big wins.

I believe that my meditation, journalling, and conscious receiving made it possible to receive financial grants for my business, compliments about my writing, opportunities to speak on conference panels, and celebratory parties for winning awards.

My Favourite Receiving Practices

1. *Regular Journaling Practice*: Develop a habit of journaling regularly to train yourself to express your thoughts and make space to receive inspiration. This practice helps clear mental clutter and opens up a channel for new ideas and creativity to flow.

2. *Practice Receiving Compliments*: When someone gives you a compliment, resist the urge to brush it off or downplay it. Instead, simply say, "Thank you." If it feels uncomfortable, use your journal to explore those feelings later. This helps you become more comfortable with positive attention and reinforces your worthiness to receive kindness.

3. *Apply for Stretch Opportunities*: Challenge yourself by applying for programs, grants, or positions that feel like a stretch. This practice pushes you out of your comfort zone and helps you become more open to receiving opportunities, recognition, and support.

4. *Meditation on Openness*: Engage in a meditation practice focused on being open to receiving. Visualize yourself as a vessel ready to receive inspiration, love, and support. The goal is to cultivate a feeling of openness and readiness to receive.

5. *Daily Gratitude Ritual*: Create a daily ritual to acknowledge and express gratitude for what you've received that day. This could be anything from a kind word to a new idea. This practice helps you recognize the abundance already present in your life and reinforces the naturalness of receiving.

6. *Engage in Supportive Conversations*: Participate in communities or groups where mutual support is encouraged. Practice sharing your needs and asking for help. This helps you become more comfortable receiving support from others and

contributes to a culture of mutual giving and receiving.

7. *Mindful Receiving of Gifts*: When receiving a gift, take a moment to fully appreciate it without immediately thinking about reciprocating. Focus on the giver's intention and allow yourself to feel gratitude and joy, reinforcing the idea that it's okay to receive without obligation.

8. *Setting Boundaries*: Practice saying no to demands that drain your energy. By setting boundaries, you create space in your life for what truly nourishes you, whether it's rest, creative inspiration, or emotional support. This practice emphasizes that receiving requires making space for it in your life.

As you embrace receiving, you'll be more open to people and experiences. You'll feel softer and more alive. You'll notice how much the universe shows up for you. You'll appreciate the little gifts as much (or more!) than the big gifts. Because they *all* feel amazing.

Then comes the shift. You open the floodgates.

More is coming at you than you want. As you get more attuned, you'll recognize the energy, people, and situations that you don't want. They're showing up or following you around or you're bumping into them and don't know how to respond. You need to bring on the boundaries and declutter that closet (so to speak).

Now you're ready to meet your feisty fairy godmother, Discernment.

Chapter Four

Discernment

B EING RECEPTIVE DOES NOT mean always saying yes. The clearer you are about what and who you want to receive, the easier it is to know what doesn't suit you. This is a vital step in being a joyful creative.

If you've spent much of your time saying yes to avoid conflict or hurt feelings, you'll find this chapter uncomfortable (at first). You'll resist what I share and insist that you can balance all the things while keeping everyone happy.

Nope. No, you won't. That, my dear friend, is fiction.

And I write fiction for a living. So, I can spot it a mile away. In other people. It's very hard to spot the need for discernment in ourselves — because that's our lesson to learn.

As we dive into the power of discernment, if you feel resistance or resentment — fabulous! You are going to recover *so* much space and energy along this path.

I have a little trick for you to use to stay engaged in this conversation. For now, use all the ideas I am sharing to spot where your neighbours, friends, sisters, employees, teachers, parents, could use some discernment. It will stand out. You won't need to go hunting or gathering to find clear examples.

The value of saying no is much easier to spot in other people's lives. The places where they could stand up for themselves, or they're people-pleasing, or they feel guilty, or they're scared to be ostracized will be incredibly obvious to you. It may hurt your heart a little or it may frustrate you.

Reminder: I am NOT asking you to do this for them. That would be called co-dependency.

Nope. I'm suggesting that you take time to notice. And without judgement, observe what might be happening over in someone else's corner. Observation and compassion can bring a soft light to places that we need to shift. With the kind of gentleness that makes a rigid resistance give a little.

What is hard to see in yourself can be painfully obvious to notice in others. And the more it irritates you? The more likely you have a similar pattern.

We came by these patterns honestly through experience and the reactions of others. The expectation that to be loved means showing up how others want you to be. Prioritizing their desires over your own.

The cumulative effect of chronically choosing others over yourself is that you suffer. Your health, your sleep, your passion projects. They all get shoved aside in service of making other people feel comfortable.

Let's be honest. Girls are still raised to please others first, be nice (as opposed to kind), and keep our opinions to ourselves. This may sound innocuous, but it *still* determines the career trajectories of famous actresses in Hollywood and multi-million-dollar singers. You can look up their videos about being bullied by film directors and executive producers when they stood up to being mistreated. The double-standard is real.

We need to stand up for the lives we want to be living, the art we want to make, the people we feel safe around, and the change we want to stand for. That is why discernment is essential to protecting your energy, wellbeing, and desires.

As a culture, we have finally begun talking about boundaries. Maybe you've had lots of conversations about setting boundaries. Or maybe you're just learning. When you've been raised without healthy boundaries or with the norm of people trampling all over them, it takes years to relearn how to protect yourself. I feel like every day is an exercise in expressing my boundaries in a kind and firm way.

Discernment is the subtle step that happens before you set those boundaries. It's about getting clear on what you need and want. It's getting to know your intuition and your unique needs. Most of your conversation with discernment will be an inner dialogue.

I recommend cultivating a practice of pausing and checking in *before* you commit to a person, event, or request. If you're more practiced (or pressured) to give an immediate response, this will take getting used to. I was a reflexive "yes-er" for a long time. Propelled by my desire to be wanted, to be included, to be liked. A lifetime of feeling left out and a highly dysfunctional family filled with criticism and little praise, created an intense desire to belong. Anywhere.

Luckily, I also have a bold fire moon that demands inner honesty. That reminded me daily that I deserve better. That my heart and creativity were priceless, and they were meant to serve what I wanted to experience and feel. That's when I discovered that this seemingly unsexy notion of discernment was the biggest power move of all.

***

Trust me, I'm aware that discernment sounds like a boring university term paper you don't want to write. Probably something about the history of footnotes and how they came to dominate the lower margins of way-too-long term papers.

BUT – don't let discernment fool you. She is a badass. In fact, she is a super-observant, deep and wise badass. She is *fierce* and intuitive and has your back. We give so much attention to assertive actions like setting boundaries.

And I believe it's equally badass to attune to our subtle powers. Like awareness, intuition, and discernment. Magical abilities that require attunement are extra potent.

We live in a time of bold, brash, and loud. When people are fighting for airwaves and attention, the subtle tools get pushed aside. Discernment doesn't tend to come up a lot. Because it's designed to feel and reveal hidden desires, quiet needs, and words that are not being said.

Which is exactly why it's more important than ever.

You may not notice her wise ways at first. When discernment first tried to get my attention, I brushed off her nudges and hints. Insisting that I was overthinking things or making a big deal out of nothing. Forcing her to get louder in my ear.

Discernment is the twin sister of Intuition. Intuition will sense what's happening under all the conversations, the exclamations, the words and promises. If someone is saying one thing and doing (or planning to do) another, Intuition sounds the alarm. Or if your mind really believes you have to go to that gathering or networking event, but your Intuition knows you are exhausted — it will tell you to stay home and replenish.

Then, discernment will pipe up. And, if you're paying attention, you'll listen close to the wisdom she's providing. She's telling you that friend is going to disappoint you again. And that event is a lot of noise that will rob your energy for tomorrow. Even though your mind might feel guilty to let that friend go. Or will insist that you're missing out that oh-so-important contact.

Except discernment knows that the quality of energy is everything. More is not better. Doing everything is not wise. Being liked by everyone is not necessary.

As you play with receiving, you want to be in environments that feel safe, uplifting, and encouraging. You want to be precious about your energy. And wise about how you spend it.

So many places and people are not worthy of your time. Let me be really clear - achieving your big, creative dreams requires discernment. Making time for yourself when you have a laundry list of to-do's requires discernment. Knowing how to say no, when you were raised to always put other's feelings first, requires discernment.

Otherwise, you'll lose your momentum and wonder -- what the heck is keeping me from reaching my dreams? From living MY life the way I want to.

You need a bold badass looking out for your best interests. For your dreams. For your sweet heart. And what she deserves. That is the role of discernment. She is your best friend, your closest advisor and ... wait for it ... your Wild Fairy Godmother.

You know - the one with fabulous outfits and a sassy mouth. She doesn't care about anyone else's needs.

She wants you to get the most out of your life. Other people's opinions be damned.

She is the whisper in your ear each time you make a choice that doesn't serve you and robs you of your clarity.

She is the nudge that reminds you that your needs matter.

She is the question that pops into your mind each time you go to an event that leaves you flat rather than lifts you up.

She is the feeling you get when everyone in your circle is excited about a conference, but you know in your heart you'd rather stay home.

As you experiment with receiving, there will be a point when you need to invite discernment to the party. Discernment is a tricky minx who dances in the subtle shades of energy.

She'll whisper in your ear that something doesn't feel quite right even though, at first glance, it seems perfect. Later, you'll notice that you never found your creative groove due to the uncomfortable chairs or the persistent cold draft from the door.

She'll encourage you to take your time back from commitments you keep purely out of habit or guilt. Insisting (again and again) that there are better ways to use that time.

Nudging you to notice one friend who lights you up and makes you feel like you can take on the world! While another friend leaves you crawling into bed and taking a nap for hours.

***

You are the steward of your energy and environment. Discernment comes into your life to assist you to take back your time. To claim your best life. To remind you that you are worth standing up for and discovering what works for YOU.

As I played with the inflow and outflow of creative energy, I inevitably bumped into the limitations. I would be excited about a new place to create, only to find that it was too dark, too loud, or just had a funky energy.

Some places radiate grumpy, cranky, cynical vibes. You know the ones. Those restaurants or cafes where you're absolutely sure that the staff gossip about each other and not one of them ever smiles. They grumble when they take your order and you end up feeling more like an imposition than a paying customer.

Or the friend that you used to love hanging around, but now you feel like all she wants to do is complain. When you meet her for a creative date, she doesn't pull out her laptop. Instead, she pulls out every story of frustration and defeat, and proceeds to tell you why the industry you're in will never let you succeed.

When I started paying attention to what lifts and emboldens me, I wanted more of that feeling. The closer I looked, the more I noticed where I was giving away my precious energy. Most of the time out of unconscious habit. Other times, it was out of guilt. And still other times, I was afraid to say no or disappoint someone.

The first steps into discernment will feel uncomfortable for anyone who identifies as a people pleaser, certified nice girl, or who forgets to ask what she wants *before* asking someone else.

Your Wild Fairy Godmother wants you to care what matters to YOU.

And while you don't have to be rude about it, she wants you to declare what works for you. Which means asking, "What *does* work for me?" "What *do* I want (really)?"

I am STILL learning to ask those questions.

And I'm STILL reminding myself that my answer may be wildly different on Thursday than it was on Monday. Which is absolutely, brilliantly perfect.

Because every moment, every day, every month is unique.

So your answer will be unique.

I'm pretty sure I was a feisty little girl who was VERY clear what she wanted. Except I was born into a family where I was the eighth person to arrive. Two parents, six kids, and a few cats.

I came along when everyone else had staked their territory and had voices and language. I had a voice, but it took me longer to get clear language. And it wasn't exactly encouraged.

So even when I was clear on *my* needs, there were seven other people who were louder, older, and had more experience asserting *theirs*. I learned to go along to get along.

In truth, I learned to go along to belong. To earn a sense of family. In a desperate attempt to feel safe and loved. That kind of training runs deep.

And requires persistent and aware de-programming.

I've realized that every bold choice that I make for me and my creations is a reclamation. Claiming who I am. What I stand for. Who I love. And what I want to do with my time.

Because every moment, word, creation, and expression matters to me.

When I was in my twenties, I felt like time was limitless. I worked hard and was incredibly determined, yet I had a sense of having all the time in the world. The older I get, the more aware I become of the finite nature of my time on this planet and with the people I care about.

Since claiming my place as a writer, storyteller, and creative entrepreneur, I've known that one of my deepest relationships and loves in this life is with my art. Whether that art is a podcast, book, conference talk, packaged food company, or community of powerful women — my creations fuel my passion for life. And add profoundly to the joy in my days.

Knowing that as a deep truth in my heart, you would think I guard my time and energy with the fierceness of a mama lion protecting her babies or a dragon guarding treasure. Ah, but early programming runs deep!

It's up to me to have a sharp eye and keen commitment to watch for sneaky ways that I relinquish my time or spend energy out of guilt rather than care.

One of my tricks is to check in after every event, gathering, meeting, or decision. It's actually quite easy. And you do it automatically, I promise. It's a simple pause where I take one or two deep breaths and ask myself. Did that give me energy or take it? Do I feel brighter and more hopeful, or do I feel tired and spent?

There are good kinds of spent and tired, like after an amazing workout. Or a long day of socialising with a favourite friend. I might feel like I have less physical or mental energy, but I also have a smile on my face, a relaxed nervous system, and I feel incredibly grateful. Those are the signs that, even though I might now need some time alone, the hours that I spent being engaged and active were well worth it.

Compare that to the times when I've gone to a dinner party because I didn't want to offend the host. I spent the evening searching for vague topics to discuss and could sense energetically that this was not a space to talk about what really matters to me. So when people ask what I do, I rarely want to give an answer because I can tell that they aren't genuinely interested.

I leave those gatherings feeling tired, sad, a little less hopeful, and wondering why the heck I agreed to go in the first place. The blessing in that experience is getting to know what works for me and what doesn't. I prefer small get-togethers with people who genuinely care about whatever it is that they're up to in the world. And more often than not, my favourite gatherings have no more than six or seven people.

And that's with my identifying as an extrovert! As an empathic extrovert, I am choosy about the people and places I want to be around. I have so much that I want to learn, see, experience, and create, that why-oh-why would I waste my time out of politeness?

With the people in my close circle, I have open conversations about how to spend quality time together and what works for each of us to be deeply connected and have fun. It's also a hella accurate way to tell if someone is committed to being close to you.

If they're not willing to have a conversation that honours your needs as well as theirs? They're not interested in a real and generous relationship. They're forcing you to adhere to their needs.

An approach that will only foster guilt and resentment, rather than closeness and love.

***

I can't possibly share about discernment without addressing where you place your attention. Attention and awareness have become absolute treasures in a time when we constantly have media and devices that want to steal it from you.

The more you give your attention to Instagram or TikTok, the less you have for your observations and inspirations. The more you give *all* your attention to outside experts, the less you have to discover what you want to learn and experience. The more you spend your attention on other people's films and TV shows and novels, the less you have to create yours.

Now. I love learning and have admired and followed many teachers. I adore TV shows and film, and I consumed thousands of them to learn the craft of screenwriting, to review films, and for pure enjoyment. I've needed the wisdom of experts in everything from astrology to meditation to recording a podcast to designing my first food label.

I absolutely, whole-heartedly need to learn from other people and their lifelong work that gives me the opportunity to leverage the brilliance and originality that was their calling. After all, I can't possibly (nor do I want to) do all the things that people put out into the world.

And — this is where discernment comes in.

Just like how after every gathering, meeting, interaction, I ask myself to feel into the energy of the experience and if it nourished me? I have learned to ask myself ~

Am I learning something important from this person? Something that empowers me and expands my perspective?

Or am I taking another course, watching another video, disappearing into a TV show because I am scared to venture out to do my own brave project? Because that means taking a stand, being original, and potentially being seen?

This is where you call on your feisty Fairy Godmother!

She will guide you in this process because it IS a process. One where you learn what works for you the more you practise. For years, I didn't realize that I was constantly asking other people to explain things to me when I could look them up or learn them faster by myself. I was so trained (that whole eighth person in the family thing) to believe that everyone else knew more than I did.

So my discerning fairy godmother gently and persistently nudged me to feel the awkwardness of trusting my judgment. To risk "getting it wrong." Except any idea that I was getting it wrong was a fallacy. Because every time I noticed that I gave away my authority, I stopped and made a different choice. A choice that trusted my intuition and judgment.

And so, I progressively claimed mine back.

Reclamation comes in little steps. Not big waves. Or crazy moves. It's a daily ritual of loving yourself deeper and knowing that you, too, came to offer the world your brilliance. And to do that, you need to feel the difference between genuine learning and avoiding sharing your gift.

It's also recognizing the difference between learning and distracting yourself.

Do you really need to take another course? Or are you avoiding the silence that's required to hear your voice? Do you really need to meet that friend today? Or are you dodging the book your heart has repeatedly asked you to start (and keep) writing? Do you really need to clean your entire kitchen before writing those email newsletters or making those phone calls?

I have been incredibly productive in my creative careers *and* I know what it feels like to prioritise everything else over my passions. For many years, I put work and pursuing my dreams in the film industry ahead of everything.

After I left, I swung in the other direction, to build community, friendships, healing, and a life that included travel. I was learning to build a marketing platform to promote my work and to be visible. Which brought some exciting and steep learning curves.

Except, I would hang out too long in the learning space (very comfortable, indeed!) instead of taking the risk of testing my ideas in the world. I would take another course or join another group instead of believing in my work.

Creative courage needs discernment as its wing woman. Because it's damn easy to hang out in spaces where we cheer other people on or learn yet another tool rather than dive into our own brave work. I thought I had to take a TON of courses in marketing, rather than writing some messaging and testing it out.

I believe in having creative supporters and collaborators. *And* I have noticed that I — and many women —feel safer learning than leading. There are SO many cultural reasons for this. Not the least of which is because we've been told over and over that our safe position is to follow, not to lead or be seen.

The interesting creative lesson for me came in recognizing that my creative work and my opportunities accelerated the braver I was. Once I left the learning circles and trusted myself ~ I felt more alive and inspired than I had felt in years. I needed the risk. And I needed discernment to tell me when I was hiding rather than learning.

There is typically a tipping point for me. If I have learned enough to get started, I need to dive in. If I stay too long, I get stuck in inertia. And it's progressively harder and scarier for me to get going.

So how do you practice discernment?

First, by creating a habit of connecting with yourself. This requires noticing how you are feeling. If you've never done this, then you could start by cultivating a meditation or a yoga practice. These are simple ways that you can get familiar with your own energy.

And if those are too stationary for you, you can do awareness walks. Preferably in a quiet area — like the forest or a park or by the water. Breathe and check in with what thoughts and emotions are cycling through you.

I love my journal for this as well. Once I clear away the surface thoughts, I always get to the rumbling feelings and/or frustrations that are underneath. The more I make this a regular practice, the easier and faster it is for me to get to anything that is holding me back.

What I love about using my journal is that it's also my space to forgive myself for choices that I regret. I've got an annoying habit of being really hard on myself for decisions that were not in my best interest. Other people would chalk this up to life lessons or learning for the next time.

My inner critic loves to give me a hell of a hard time - for WAY too long - over minor infractions. I suspect this comes from being raised in a home rife with criticism while offering minimal praise.

To cultivate self-compassion, I built a forgiveness practice as a consistent habit. I needed the loving acceptance that I found in my journal pages. By simply writing out in dramatic detail all my feelings, thoughts, and frustrations about a situation.

The more honest I was, the deeper the kindness that appeared on the other side. The kind of generous acceptance I would give a close friend. It's that kind of acceptance that creates space for discernment. For those gorgeous a-ha moments filled with revelation. The ones that deliver the answer you needed about a friend, an offer, a job, and all the other big (and little) decisions.

The more that you cultivate awareness, the easier it will be for you to feel the subtle differences between situations that are supportive of you, and the ones that are stealing your power.

My greatest lessons in discernment have come through relationships. Friendships, colleagues, bosses, family members. I was raised to give a lot of grace to other people without expecting the same in return. This was courtesy of being raised in a family with active addiction (hello, co-dependence) and heavy-duty Christian programming. This seemed to apply to the girls in the family. Not so much the boys.

As I grew into adult relationships, I felt hard-wired to let people get away with a LOT of bad behaviour. Especially women. I had hard boundaries with men because I valued my physical safety above all else. I grew up with physical abuse and was unwilling to be around it or near it.

My boundaries with women took a LOT longer. I was very confused by people who said one thing and did another. Which seemed to be a common tactic among women. My closest and dearest male friend taught me a lot about what I deserved. As I've grown older, I've paid MUCH closer attention to people who expect a lot of grace, understanding and forgiveness but are unwilling to give it to me. I have family members who expected me to show up for them emotionally, physically, and financially but had absolutely no intention of doing that for me.

That kind of mistreatment undermines personal confidence and self-esteem. I began weeding those people out of my life. Much like I would weed my garden. And the most beautiful result happened. While I grieved and felt lonely for a while, I felt stronger. I liked myself more. I found friends who wanted to support me and cheer me on and show up.

That made it even easier to see the people who didn't operate with kindness and generosity. And I could feel how draining it was to be around them. Minimizing contact made it easier to love myself. Even wilder? My dreams began blossoming! Removing the energy drains from my life made room for dreams and goals and true friendship to thrive.

***

Now, I aspire to have a life that I love while giving my best creative energy to my projects *first*. Do I wake up every morning at 5am? Heck no! But I do know that when I meditate and work out first thing, I have a clear mind, heart and body to write what I really want to say.

And I do my writing first. If I need to get up earlier to accomplish those words, I do. I'm not a write every day kind of gal (at least, not in a long time), *but* I create every day. I make sure that I am fuelling my heart — and feeling connected to my creative joy. Because when I prioritise my creative expression, I am a happier, more generous, more exuberant human being.

When I don't? All that creative energy gets hella grumpy. I become resentful, jealous, and all the other feelings that simmer to a boil when a creative person ignores her gifts.

The biggest reason that I adore discernment for all her uncomfortable life lessons is -- when I heed her wisdom, I discover that I have a lot of time.

Time for what matters. Time for what nourishes me. Time for the people and communities that are important. Time for the messages, stories, love, and humour that matter to me.

I remind myself that the people in my life who truly love and support me will understand when I can't come to every event, or meet everyone for that drink, or need some extra time at home (or in New York City). They may feel disappointment, but they don't let it impact our friendship.

And I make sure that I do the same for them when a visit gets cancelled or a trip can't happen. I remember that we all need to make choices to live our best lives.

Make a commitment to invite your discerning fairy godmother into your creative life. If you're just getting started with making choices that put your work ahead of others or ahead of cleaning your home, know that every uncomfortable moment pays huge dividends.

You'll see traction in your projects. You'll feel proud. You'll feel less of a pull to take care of others or look perfect … and you'll pour that energy into creative endeavours that reflect who you are and what you *really* want.

After all, you came here to learn, make, explore, dance, sing, and much more. You have a limited amount of time and energy. Bringing discernment onto your team will exponentially increase the time you have to express what's truly on your heart.

And once you get used to it?

You'll love the feeling of choosing YOU more and more. Until each time you do it, you'll discover a lovely smile on your face. And a shimmer of joy in your heart.

Chapter Five

Inspiration

A FTER PRIMING MY RECEPTIVITY, I know when I'm ready for inspiration. I want ideas to come. I feel rested and clear enough to be curious.

Without rest and recuperation, I am too tired to care. Too spent to connect. It's like my creative intuition knows that there just isn't enough gas in the tank to go the distance, so why even try?

But once I have some gas in the tank? Look out! I love the rush that comes when an idea lights me up inside. The cascade of inspiration begins like a rush of water finding a cliff and turning into a waterfall. Or, if I am still a bit on the tired side, a solid trickle.

Either way, I'll take it!

Inspiration feels fleeting and magical. Like a cheeky fairy that swoops in to sprinkle idea dust then swoops away. If you're not paying attention, you'll think it was a spring breeze. Or a car whooshing by. Instead of the magical instigator that came to play only to find me asleep at the keyboard.

While the last two practices — receiving and discernment — were softer and more feminine, inspiration requires more active seeking. When I spend too much time in the same room, the same routine, drinking the same coffee, and staring at the same walls? Inspiration falls asleep.

Yes, she can find me. But typically, it's a half-hearted affair, tinged with the same muted shades of mediocre enthusiasm. Inspiration likes to be played with, courted, sought out, and chased. She's a sprightly wee air spirit that wants engagement.

So when I know that I'm deflated and less than enthusiastic about my work, I know it's time to stir the pot and get out and about! Air spirits need movement. Ideas need fresh energy!

In case you wonder why I keep going on about air, the word inspiration comes from the Latin root, *inspiratus*, meaning, "to breathe into." Many folks have translated that to mean the breath of God or Divine guidance.

Inspiration is the breath of spirit going through us. It comes through many channels. Directly when we're alone in the car, at our desk, or in the woods. Collectively, when we're tossing ideas around with friends and fellow creatives. Spontaneously, when we're watching a movie, eavesdropping in a cafe, or staring up at the moon.

So when you feel inspired, you're being lifted by the winds of the Divine. Filled with vibrant oxygen and prepared either to take flight or catch fire. Choose your preferred metaphor.

Inspiration is a partner in the receiving process. That's why we need to be so determined and committed to making space. If your head and calendar and time are so jam-packed with running around and doing things and obsessing about details, how would Inspiration possibly get through all that noise?

I've begun actively cultivating times of silence. I'm someone who typically packs WAY too much into her day. Always learning something more. Meeting someone new. Joining another call. Reading another book. Responding to a request.

Until I feel heavy and bloated with everyone else's ideas. If my inspiration fairies have been buzzing around looking for an opening, they definitely wouldn't find one. And I get grumpy and wonder why no new ideas had arrived.

Easy fix! I was making absolutely no quiet time or intentional space for them. It's a reflex for me to put on a podcast or audiobook when I'm in the car. So, I had to interrupt that habit consciously and create one of quiet when I'm driving. It's hella uncomfortable.

I kept wanting to reach for my phone. To chat with someone or leave a message. Instead, when I take time to breathe and relax, it's wild how quickly my mind goes into curious mode.

If you're like me, I guarantee the first few attempts at silence will make you twitchy. Whether you need it in the car, at lunch, on a walk, or in the bath. Silence is a sparkling sign to your muse fairies that you are exhaling all the information swirling around your mind. And instead, you're exhaling. Relaxing. Priming your receptors.

Think about the times that your muse swoops in, when you least expect her, and sprinkles you with idea dust. When I got curious about this phenomenon, I saw the connection quickly.

The times when my muse appears tend to be:

~ In the car.

~ On a walk.

~ When I'm first waking up.

~ In the middle of the night.

~ When I first drift off to sleep.

~ In the shower.

~ On the subway.

~ Doing laundry, dishes, vacuuming, etc.

~ Simple tasks like stacking wood or raking leaves.

~ During a boring talk or Zoom call.

~ While meditating or journalling.

~ Sitting quietly in a café.

~ People watching in any city.

All times when I've let go and am in a relaxed (almost meditative) state. When I am not pushing. Not expecting. Not trying to make something happen. I'm open and available.

I love when ideas come to me this way. Even though it's damn inconvenient if I need a journal and my hands are wet. I still love it because receiving ideas this way, after all these years, feels like magic.

It reminds me of two things — that I need to show up and be willing. And I need to make space for inspiration to show up.

When being creative is a daily endeavour, it's easy to forget that it's meant to be playful. And once it's attached to income or money? It's even easier to turn it into a burden or chore instead of remembering that the whole thing is a playful game.

The lighter my hold on my creative efforts, the more enjoyable the whole thing is. And the faster the ideas fly to me. Like inspiration knows I'm up for anything and that's WAY more fun for everyone. The trickster fairy gets to swoosh and swoop and play loose with the rules.

Like we did when we were little ones.

Which leads me to my next point. When I was little, I showed up every day with a willing heart and bold excitement. I didn't grumble and groan and expect inspiration to find me sitting in my cranky pants. I bounced outside in my imaginary cape and was ready to roll!

I suspect that many creatives, myself included, fall into the trap of expecting inspiration to find us. While that is how it works, I *also* believe we need to meet inspiration. It makes all the difference when I go out into the world, open my eyes (and heart), and actively look around.

It's like Inspiration realizes that I'm committed. I've put myself out there. Like a gal who's decided that she's ready to date again and the idea suitors come calling. Only in this case, it's a cheeky inspiration fairy wanting to lead me astray on all kinds of winding creative paths.

If you find yourself mired and stuck and without fresh ideas, odds are you've been staring at the same four walls, hanging around the same person, ignoring your nudges to get you outside and breathing new or fresh air, and forgetting to give yourself the essential gift of newness ... to have fresh thoughts, notions, connections, and energy.

I suspect that inspiration is the air element — and moves as fast as a dragonfly. Darting this way and that to catch our fancy. We need to explore it and dance with it for a while to get a sense of whether the inspiration will last. That moment needs inspiration to dance with the spark of passion for a project to have the energy to sustain through the challenging parts.

But I'm getting ahead of myself! I'll talk about the spark in Chapter Six, *Sparks*.

Before the WHOOSH that comes when a spark ignites, you need time to play.

Many of us do our initial creative work alone. Whether you are a writer, graphic designer, or architect, you spend a lot of solo time with your creative genius. With that in mind, I suggest inspirational activities that are contradictory to how you spend your creative production time.

Discovering a fresh view, person, conversation, feeling, or piece of art initiates the dialogue with inspiration. Ideas that wouldn't happen without the mischievous act of stepping away from routine. That's when a wondrous idea arrives on the wings of fairies ~ activating the next leap of your project.

Anne Lamott (author of *Bird by Bird*) put it like this: "Almost everything will work again if you unplug it for a few minutes, including you."

I dare you to unplug for more than a few minutes and make a habit of chatting with inspiration. You were never meant to create all alone - and the process is more joyful, elegant, and efficient when you treat sourcing inspiration as a regular ingredient in your creative process.

Sourcing inspiration fuels your creative production. I highly recommend shifting your creative mindset about taking inspiration "breaks." Creative flow needs movement. Inspiration needs air. I swear it arrives on the wings of fairies and spirits. And if you are stuck in a chair in front of a laptop for too long, they all fly away and you're left with the same old stagnant ideas.

Okay. That might be overstating it a little. But — I firmly believe that to be inspired and curious creators, we need to partake of many sources. Poetry, graffiti, airplane rides, and spontaneous conversations with strangers. These are the magical sources of inspiration that cultivate ideas all around the world.

Like a magical network of notions flitting around for each of us to grab. Very possibly being delivered by our Divine Geniuses like a collective steno pool behind the scenes that we will never see, but we feel the impact and are whisked back to our desks to capture the brilliance that flies through our fingers.

There are days when inspiration is whooshing through me like a gale force wind or a tornado that needs to be caught by the tail and wrestled onto a page. Then there are days when nary a breeze can be found. I'm standing at my desk wondering why the air doesn't seem to move and nothing has stirred my heart enough to provoke words or visual expression.

While I love the days when taking a shower stirs the currents of inspiration, or I wake up having dreamed half of what I will write for the day, there are just as many times that I recognize that the winds of inspiration need to be stirred. That I can't rely on the breeze arriving on its own.

Just as we need to commit to the creative habit of showing up for our work, we need to commit to sourcing inspiration. Treating our creativity with the same respect that we give to other relationships in our life. Take your creative genius out for some fun!

You cannot possibly expect her to deliver consistently when all she has seen is the inside of your kitchen — where you make the same cup of tea every day.

Those are the times when I imagine that inspiration is a fairy minx that eludes me purposefully to shake up my routine, connect me to other creatives, and get outside the little box of my brain to consider fresh ideas, spaces, and thoughts.

No. That is an inhumane handling of a mystical force that is designed to prod you out into the world to receive fresh insight. I often imagine my creative genius as not one, but three saucy and irreverent muses who have a LOT to say about my creative routine.

They gather and toss acerbic opinions back and forth while smoking and rolling their eyes at my boring routines. If they could, they would toss me on an airplane every week so that I could experience the full beauty and awe of being on the earth. Wanting me to drink in the essence of being alive what it is to be a creative human being.

I love my lippy muses. They make me laugh. And they spur me to try things that I would never do. They remind me to have a sense of humour about myself and my process. Even better, they tell me that creating is meant to be dynamic and unpredictable and fun. That inspiration is found in the most unlikely and unusual places. So why wouldn't I seek them out?

While they know that I have a vivid imagination, they want to challenge it. They want me to see and feel and be amazed by the brilliance of OTHER creatives who have totally different talents to mine. Who see the world through different eyes and who can shake up how I might write my next story or spin my next podcast idea.

Inspiration is meant to be surprising. To take us off guard. To whisk us off our feet when we're driving along, catching sight of a new billboard or hearing a song for the first time. When this happens, we feel the rush of being alive all over again. And we are reborn.

***

I am infinitely grateful that I discovered the film industry at the beginning of my creative career. From the beginning, that art form is understood to be a collaborative art. The expectation is set that the writer creates the script, which then goes to a producer, who then hires a director and actors. The story is filmed by a crew of ten or one hundred, possibly in multiple locations.

Then it experiences the creative process of post-production, where the story is told again in the editing suite and has music and effects added. Even though, as a writer, I didn't necessarily get to work directly with all that creative talent, I knew that my words were only the beginning.

When I shifted from being a screenwriter to being a novelist, I ran *smack* into the cultural paradigm of the *lone artist*, struggling away with her story until she got it right. Wrestling with the words, her demons, and all the expectations of carrying the burden of being a sole creative genius. UGH.

No, thank you. The only part of that I was even remotely interested in was that I got to expand the structure, genre, and wordplay that came into my novels. I also got to write stories that shook up cultural norms and put strong women at the heart of the tale.

But when it came to the writing, editing, designing, and marketing? I made damn sure that I brought along my best friend from the film business, and soon created a trio of powerful creators. Our intention was to support one another in our daring adventure of writing the stories of our hearts and diving into the foray of publishing.

I cannot imagine editing my own words or designing the book cover or doing the layout for the paperback. I craved having a team. To empower other creative geniuses to do their best work and have fun while doing it. I never believed that I was supposed to create *and* put together all the pieces.

Working closely with other creatives is a powerful source of inspiration. In our creative, empathic sharing, we fuel each other. We bring our geniuses together and, much like a mastermind, become multipliers of each other's talent.

I believe in finding inspiration in the art and expression of others – in podcasts, books, movies, and talks. I certainly consume my fair share of all these inspiring expressions. They spark ideas and curiosity and break through many limiting beliefs through their creative alchemy. I'll share more about that practice in the coming chapters.

Somewhere along the creative evolutionary trail, we decided that we're meant to forge creative ideas alone and refuse any notion of collaboration. That we are the primary creative force. Everything is coming from our little minds (as opposed to through us) and that surrounding ourselves with creative geniuses and provocateurs would jeopardize our ideas.

In a nutshell, we were convinced that to be a REAL artist, you must toil alone. Stay alone. Protect your art alone. Anything else will compromise the vision, open you up to theft, or even worse - reveal that you just couldn't hack doing it *alone*. Also known as, "you're not a real artist if you have help."

Rugged individualism got mixed in with the artist archetype and became the dominant artistic culture. Our human myopia took hold of a process that has always been a sacred partnership between an individual and the cosmic forces. Whether you consider that force energy, God, the universe, collective consciousness, or a myriad of other names.

Elizabeth Gilbert shares a little of this perspective in her brilliant TED talk, *Your Elusive Creative Genius*.

"In ancient Greece and ancient Rome, people did not happen to believe that creativity came from human beings. People believed that creativity was this divine attendant spirit that came to human beings from some distant and unknowable source, for distant and unknowable reasons ... So the ancient artist was protected from certain things, like, for example, too much narcissism, right? If your work was brilliant, you couldn't take all the credit for it. Everybody knew that you had this disembodied genius who had helped you."

My strongest moments of inspiration come when I pause and connect. Talking with my friends. Wandering down a street, listening to the birds. Noticing the unique pattern of leaves on a tree. Feeling the wind on my face. The nudge to take a random turn on a street that I wouldn't normally walk.

I'm grateful for the revelations that come when reading a book. But if I am searching for my unique expression, I need to be conversing with my muse. And that requires space. Quiet. Time for ideas to drop in. For associations to be made. And curious questions to surface.

We rarely make space for quiet these days. I believe it's an essential ingredient for inspiration.

How would you hear your muse whispering in your ear? When would you have room to allow a fresh notion to occur to you? How could you hear your voice over the din of everyone else's?

Stepping away from your work can feel counterintuitive as a productivity trick. But speaking as someone who has perpetual ants in her pants, I can attest to the amazing ideas and edits that arrive when I step away from what writers call my latest WIP (work in progress).

When I keep pushing in an aggressively productive way, the space for inspiration gets smaller and smaller. Like I am cutting off the channel. But when I take a step back and breathe, I go into receptive mode. I open up. I make space for fresh energy and a-ha moments.

I swear that when I step *away* from my desk, my muses snap awake. They perk up from their lounging positions (on a very comfortable and muse-y couch) and realize that I am open. When I'm at my desk, my mind is in intense analytic mode. Putting the puzzle pieces of a creative project together. I love this part of me, it's fun and clever and determined.

And when I get up and step away from my laptop, I release the intense use of my analytic mind, relax, and open my psyche. My muses can tell that I've shifted from methodical to reflective mode. The intense focus lets go, and there's a lot more space around my attention.

They get up from that loungy couch and, from a distance like attentive cats, track what I am doing. Curious whether this state will last longer than ten minutes. My muses follow me looking for an opening. Or maybe I *finally* relax long enough to get curious.

Doing a routine task makes all kinds of room for inspiration to swoop in on a magic carpet. Or in my case, delivered by a room of chic and opinionated muses.

The routine aspect of this inspiration trick is key. You're doing something that doesn't require much of your conscious mind. Boiling the kettle, driving the car on a familiar route, strolling down a road you would know blindfolded ~ puts you in a relaxed and receptive state.

I'm still working on my WIP while I am making that tea or picking up my mail, so I'm in both crafting mode and inspiration mode. How magical is that? When you build this habit into your creative rhythm, you're consistently inviting your muse to the party. So, you'll discover better ideas!

I often realize that I've taken the easy or cliché route with a story. And I thank my lucky stars that I saw the limitation before I committed to the dang thing! Saving myself heartbreak and oodles of editing time.

This is where added efficiency and mindset comes in. Even though I am away from my laptop, I often get better ideas or fix a snag in my story with a simple walk down the street.

I am trading a fifteen-minute break (also better for my body and mind - bonus!) for days or weeks of frustration in edits. Or the times I catch myself starting something in my business that was to entertain me but, truthfully, didn't serve my customers. A costly misstep that a LOT of entrepreneurs make when they're feeling bored or frustrated or hemmed in by their business.

The other element in this approach is inviting play into your creative process. Remember play? That crazy and fun creative partner who always has the kookiest ideas and verges on upsetting the apple cart, yet makes the day fly by in a flash?

Play makes our days fun ... a notion that got hammered out of me in service of word counts, productivity sprints, and every other pushy tactic to meet the industrial revolution's idea of a worthy day's work. And yet. Creativity thrives on fun.

Before I take this too far, you know that I believe in creative commitment and healthy habits. I secretly believe that commitment and fun are the best of friends. A hilarious pairing like Garfield and Nermal, Ernie and Bert, Jane Fonda and Lily Tomlin. That to be their best, fun and commitment need each other.

Yet, somewhere along the way, entrepreneurial culture focused way too much on the productive commitment side of things and forgot all about fun. Play. Silliness. Wild notions. Why do you think we all love the Einstein quote that liberates us from our serious mind-traps: "Creativity is intelligence having fun."

When I take myself or my work a wee bit too seriously, inspiration leaves the room. Probably because I have locked myself into a tight box of what is acceptable and not acceptable. And if you've noticed, inspiration is definitely *not* a fan of boxes.

Inspiration needs room, air, sunshine, and movement. So, I implore you - weave sunlight and fairy dust into your days. Dance. Move. Get outside. Laugh with a friend. Stroll down a country road. Make space for the brilliant fairy muses that want to deliver ideas to you. Or the cranky, snarky, loungy, creative muses. Every muse is wonderful and primed to deliver ideas your way.

I love imagining them following me around. Debating who gets to lob the idea this time. Or maybe even joking about how obscure and obtuse they want to be. I imagine that working with me can be hella frustrating. I have a stubborn streak. Which is great for getting projects completed. But not so great for welcoming fresh notions.

Heck. That's half the reason I figure they need to repeat themselves. Ideas swoosh in and swoosh out. Sometimes I grab them and act. Sometimes I think, how amazing! And move along.

My muses can get worked up when I am having an excitable day. Lobbing all kinds of notions my way. Who knows? Maybe they have a betting pool going as to whose idea will actually make it to the next stage. And the thrill of so many ideas is like candy to my creative soul.

To be fair, it's important for me to stay focused on what I want to get done. Not get distracted by every notion that comes along. Deadlines and milestones are key to completing a project. Whether you have an external deadline or a self-determined one. They keep us inspired and moving.

But I've learned to soften about deadlines over the years. Especially since writing my second book, *Blue Moon*. I love that book, and I've returned to the story for a sequel. And still, I feel like when I wrote the story, I may have done it a disservice.

I wrote that novel when cranking books out quickly was thought to be the only way to build a profitable career as an author. I was gifted this story and the characters by my eloquent muses. It's a wild tale set in New York City with the three sisters of fate. They discover that to stop a shadowy force from causing havoc, they have to seek the help of a rather impetuous human, Helen.

While writing, I became determined to force the book to be ready by a certain date. The more stubborn I got, the less time I made to hang out with the characters. I stopped checking that I was enjoying the process and was respecting the way the story wanted to be told. I got deadline-obsessed. Believing that real authors wrote quickly. And moved on to the next book.

Some authors write quickly. Maybe you're one of them. I am sometimes, too. And sometimes, I need to allow the best book to come forth. Because when I write, I'm learning, too. I'm evolving. I'm following a story or an idea that is meant to change me, then change the reader. And that is a sacred journey that doesn't always adhere to a human clock.

At least, not the same way that I predict it will. Magic has its own timeline. And the longer I create, the more magic I want to experience. The more magic I want to weave into my creations and into the world. I trust that weaving magic is the main reason that I do what I do.

Forcing Blue Moon to be complete before it was ready did a disservice to the story, the characters, and me. The great thing about learning to be more flexible? I can return to that tale and take another swing at it.

As you progress in your next endeavour, stop to ask:

~ How can I invite enthusiasm into my process?
~ Do I need to get up, breathe, and take a break?
~ Does this feel forced?
~ Has the joy evaporated from the room?
~ What does magic feel like to me?
~ If I created more space, what might happen?

If the answers aren't coming, take these questions for a walk or a drive. Or into your journal.

Set aside your analytical mind and make room for the answers to show up. When you pause, you'll be surprised what shows up to support you.

Inspiration is a dialogue with the Divine. Allowing the conversation to come to you by being quiet and open. There is a second stage to the inspiration process that varies from pure inspiration. It's a proactive dialogue with the world.

And it's called, *stimulus.*

Chapter Six

Stimulus

I BELIEVE INSPIRATION IS the whisper of our muses. Our conduit to the Divine. That magical, mystical experience when ideas come out of the blue.

Stimulus, on the other hand, is seeking energy from the world. It's an active decision to connect with the beauty, art, and energy around you. Just as we need ideas from magical muses, we also need energy from being out in the world.

Inspiration gets us excited and moves us forward. That rush of air swoops over a spark inside us. When you interact with the world, that energy stokes the fire. Like blowing on an ember and getting the first flames burning.

As creatives, we need places, people, events, and creative works that give us energy. When I walk into a favourite store, for example, it's because every item in that store tends the fire in my heart. I need to see colours, hear music, notice textures, admire a skill that I don't have, and wonder whether I need another candle in my office.

It's like the creative part of me feels what went into making every item. And the sheer sensual delight of it all stirs the creative embers. I'm receiving vitality on every level. From sensual – through my senses – to energetic to mythical and symbolic.

Active stimulus is a key element in a joyfully creative reality. I don't finish creative projects by holing myself up away from the world for eight weeks, avoiding all contact with others and ignoring everything around me. That may work for a tiny sliver of the creative population, but the vast majority of us are social creatures that need the delightful input that light up our creative mind.

I don't pretend to fully understand how it works. But I do know that I am fuelled by the upbeat energy of others in a coffee shop. Just hearing the buzz of conversation around me gives me the rush to write faster. And the delightful whimsy of journals, signs, candy, handmade felt animals, and dozens of ever-changing products in my favourite store, fills my heart with joy.

***

When I feel empty of creative ideas and energy, I end up tired or frustrated. Those are my indicators that I need to get out of the house and experience a fresh view, place, person, or other stimuli. Even the drive (or scooter ride!) is stimulating. The movement, views, other people on the road, wondering where I want to go, and exploring a new area brings fresh energy.

Depending on how you're wired, you might need to go sit by the ocean. Or walk deep into a forest. Those are really restorative and bring inspiration. I live surrounded by nature (it's that essential to my well-being). So while I find the forest restorative, I need to go be around people and in towns to get my refill of fun and delight.

I think of creative energy as a well or a fuel tank. The longer I'm working on my WIP, the lower the tank goes. I feel sluggish and my productivity slows down. And the repetitive stance and environment make my ideas kind of lazy.

I get stuck and it gets harder to find fresh perspectives. Sometimes, I go around and around without realizing how much mental drive I am wasting. That's typically the point when my partner tells me that I look like I'm going stir-crazy (or cross-eyed from staring at my screen too long). And quickly sends me on a joyride.

I aim to be proactive about my replenishment. Because the more depleted my tank gets, the more entrenched I get

KATE TREMILLS

in my work. Making it all the harder to thrust me out of the house. It's like my intelligence turns off and I switch into "slog mode." Thinking that if I just push harder, somehow the ideas that haven't been coming for over an hour will miraculously break through.

Nope. Doesn't happen. Totally works the other way.

The longer that I insist on creative trudging, the slower the idea train becomes. Making the whole thing tortuous, rather than free-flowing and joyful.

You don't want that. Trust me. It's excruciating. I'd bet money you've been to the hellish creative train stop called, "Fraud Station." Where your mind starts screeching, "Where the eff have my ideas gone? Did I ever have any talent?" And berating you with notions of imposteritis and self-doubtus maximus. Afflictions that haunt everyone who ends up at that torturous pitstop.

Avoid that place! Make it a proactive creative habit to seek fresh views and energy.

This commitment to my joy always pays dividends. I have yet to go out and think, "Well that was a total waste of time." Unless I end up stuck in traffic and never reach my destination. And that's happened only once or twice in my many, many outings.

***

Discovering that I couldn't stay in my home and expect ideas to seek me out came as a little bit of a surprise. I thought that if I just showed up to my desk and laptop every day, inspiration would *find me* and I could merrily produce whatever script or book or article I wanted.

Except, inevitably the energy ran out. I lost my direction. I lost my motivation. And I probably turned into what I affectionately call, A Grumpy Ass. This happened even faster when I wasn't working on a few projects at once.

I was FAR more productive and inspired when I was working as a consultant and writing screenplays and meeting up with fellow authors and imagining new business ideas. I suspect it's because those activities got me out of the house and interacting with fun and interesting people, cafes, and neighbourhoods.

Now, some of this is because, along the merry path of my creative endeavours, I had a wild and confronting revelation. After decades of believing that I was a full-tilt, DEEP introvert, like the rest of my family, my partner made a declaration that I *immediately* denied.

What was this heinous proclamation? That I, Kate Tremills, was an extrovert.

Wait, WHAT?

"Nope. No way. You're crazy. Unh uh," was my response. All the while feeling that intuitive tap on my shoulder saying, "Ummmm. He's right."

Like most of my partner's crazy notions, they grab hold and take root soon after he's declared them. This one was no different. Except it flew in the face of my self-image. My identity as a writer (*all writers are introverts, right?*), my understanding of my family (*who love reading and are homebodies*), and my confusion about what it really means to be an introvert or extrovert.

When the notion took hold, I began a search for understanding. In that search, I quickly came across the definition of sourcing your energy. Introverts do it by being alone (inner sourcing). While extroverts source energy from being out in the world (external sourcing).

This idea explained confusion I'd had for a while. Why was it that when I spent too much time at home, alone, or with my WIP (work in progress), I began to feel deflated. Tired. Worn out. I used to spend oodles of time by myself!

Except, when I looked at it honestly, I realized that I grew up in a house filled with eight people, two or three cats, and a dog. When I went to university, I almost always lived with someone.

For years before the pandemic of 2020, I consulted inside companies and had a vibrant creative life with my writers groups and film friends. Even my cycling life was in groups (though, to be fair, that was a new phenomenon for me after being a solo runner for years).

At the time that I wondered why I was running out of creative steam, I had been working from home, writing my novels alone, and had a partner who was super-busy running a bike store. I spent a LOT of time by myself.

This — and the extrovert proclamation — got me looking back at my time in the film industry. I really missed the camaraderie and collaborative creativity. How had I ended up in a scenario where I was doing almost everything by myself? With little to no fresh stimulus or people?

I started experimenting with getting out of my house — writing in coffee shops. Going to different neighbourhoods and trying out fresh scenery. Meeting up with friends as an essential part of being an energised and connected person. I noted that I (mostly) felt a lot better after a boost of spending time around people or with my favourite people.

Through a series of experiments, I discovered that there was a spectrum to being an introvert/ extrovert. I am actually pretty close to the centre. Or so says the Myers Briggs test. I am also highly sensitive. So, unlike a lot of extroverts, I don't like crowds, big parties, loud entertainment, busy places, or talking about pretty much anything.

I'm definitely an alchemy between an introvert and extrovert. I absolutely love my creative alone time. I now see, however, that if I go to a favourite café (and yes, I am selective about which one) with a fellow creative and we chat for a bit then get down to work? I am wildly productive! The doubling down of focus between us makes for an amazing ride.

I bring all of this up because I believe that stimulation is absolutely essential to being a joyful creative. If inspiration is air, stimulation is fire. We need inspiration like we need oxygen. And we need stimulation to spark the creative engine.

Both introverts and extroverts need stimulation. We need the energy that the world gives us. We may just need it in different quantities or various rhythms. Staying in our own little realm can lead to a slightly myopic view.

This begs the question: what ignites your creative spark? What lights you up? What gets you writing or brainstorming in an easy flow?

Too much insular living can lead to a slump in energy and enthusiasm, no matter whether you are an introvert or an extrovert.

Some days, I have no interest in conversation with people. But I want to be outside, listening to the ravens or ocean or window displays of a nearby town (trust me, they are chatty and have a LOT of opinions. Especially the window displays for bookstores). I need someone else's expression to spark my own. To get me stretching my assumptions and personal experience.

The definition of stimulation says, "arousing interest, enthusiasm and excitement."

So not inspiration — where ideas come in and flow through you. Instead, stimulation fills your energy tank. Gets you excited. They are related. Very likely twin sisters. But there is a difference between an idea coming to and through you and a need to be revved up and excited!

I've discovered that if I get out of my home once a day, it changes my energy. I get restless and distracted if I stay in my house all day. I can manage staying home for a day. But after one, it turns into diminished enthusiasm the next day. Even less the day after that.

That's not to say that is your stimulation rhythm. You might be perfectly happy to be at home for three days in a row. I would just ask that you check in and see if you're becoming stuck or frustrated or grumpy. My partner is perfectly happy being at home for a few days and has gone as long as a week. But his viewpoint gets increasingly limited. He stops reaching for brighter, bolder ideas. And even though he loves his own company, he gets a bit insular.

I advocate for you to seek provoking environments that are *specifically* going to give you creative energy. Being around collaborative people (like in cafes or fun discussions) or creative events (like a concert or art show or farmer's market).

Places filled with a creative buzz — that will spark ideas and inspiration. Being in these places jump-starts your receptivity and fills you with the kind of energy that comes from being in the world.

And if, like me, you're sensitive to the energy of a place or people, finding your happy places will take some experimenting. I love creating in cafes, but even though I am surrounded by coffee shops, I drive thirty minutes to my preferred spot. I probably pass at least twenty cafes along the way to where I like to write.

My favourite place? A café that has big, bright rooms. Windows that reach floor to ceiling. The staff are delightful, kind, and warm. They're happy to see me typing away for two hours. Sunshine streams in, but it's not too hot. The open space means that while I hear the soft din of other people's conversations. They aren't locked in by low ceilings making them sound harsh.

And they make a heck of a cappuccino.

Even the manager was surprised to hear that I drove thirty minutes from home to work in their little spot. But when I do? My day goes so much better – I am a happier writer. The bonus is that I often receive inspiration on the drive. In the last few months, I also added the Monday morning commitment of meeting my long-time writing friend to the mix. We chat for twenty minutes, then dive into writing. Riding the wave of each other's creative energy.

I believe that writing in a café gives me the juice to write faster and with more enthusiasm. I'm surrounded by people who inspire my stories. And, even though my work is solitary, I'm being buoyed by the world.

I'm not alone when it comes to designers and writers who prefer to spend time in cafés. I have many friends who do the same – riding the wave of energy to finish deadlines or push through another stage of their project.

I've heard many speculations about why we are drawn to working in cafes – from the notion that it creates a deadline (the time window we have there) or makes us feel self-conscious if we aren't working on something. Maybe that negative mindset works for some folks.

I find (as does Malcolm Gladwell) that being in a café surrounds me with a joyful, buoyant energy. Some of the writers famously known for working in cafes are J.K. Rowling, Gertrude Stein, Natalie Goldberg, Ian Ranking, and Malcolm Gladwell. Gladwell used coffee shops to recreate the buzz and noise of the newsroom, where he got his start as a writer.

Natalie Goldberg speaks about another reason why being surrounded by people is essential. As a writer, you're hearing the flow of words and expressions that go into your work. She said, "writing is ninety percent listening.

You listen so deeply to the space around you that it fills you, and when you write, it pours out of you."

You're connected to the real world and, even if it's only by osmosis, you're capturing the true way that people feel and speak. This is true whether you're a writer, painter, course facilitator, intuitive medium, or website designer. Being around the people that you're serving makes a huge difference in your energy and the quality of your work.

I've heard Malcolm Gladwell make fun of the writer in the café. And while I appreciate the humour in his Wall Street Journal article, "*The Jerk at the Café, C'est Moi*," there are many of us who are mindful of supporting our local cafés.

We're kind to the staff. We consider how long we're at a table. We smile kindly at fellow writers and designers while enjoying being out in the wild. We clear our own dishes and are sure to tip. You choose how you interact with your community, whether that's a café owner or entrepreneurs. Which cultivates the bright and kind energy that you want to experience.

Another surprise was that when I gather my favourite creators to enjoy a coffee while brainstorming or working side by side? It doubles my joy *and* my creative output. Often, I write more words and receive more ideas. I'm simultaneously getting the wonderful input of the café, while connecting with dear friends.

The next time you're sidling up to a table at your favourite spot, you may make a new friend. Or bring a boost of encouragement to a lone creative who caught the delight in your smile as you sit at your own tables. Sharing the pleasure of company while you focus on your work.

***

The tricky part with seeking Stimulus is that it's sneakily close to its cousin, Distraction.

So I'm calling our fairy godmother Discernment back for this chat. I need discernment to help tell the difference between stimulation that replenishes my creativity and distraction that sends me down hours long rabbit holes and leaves me spent.

I rarely make unequivocal statements but I am making one about your phone and social media. Taking time on social or scrolling on your phone is not a healthy stimulus habit. They rob my attention and deplete my ideas. Blurring the line between what I want to make and what's already out there. Plus, they can stir up that nasty condition - Comparisonitis.

I am deplorably guilty of grabbing my phone on lunch breaks, walk breaks, bathroom breaks. Yup. Pretty much any time that I'm away from doing my creating. I know how frickin' addictive that damn thing is. And how easy it is to grab it and feel like you're being replenished.

But you really aren't. At least, not the kind that makes you feel lit up and refreshed when you return to your desk. So, I err on the side of outside adventures. Rather than consuming what other people have posted.

My other practice is to pay really close attention to my mood and my thoughts. I check in before and after any activity. Taking time to notice whether I have more excitement and ideas or am I feeling cranky and tired. Am I feeling inspired or anxious?

This wasn't clear at first. But like anything, when I consistently observed my thoughts and mood after a joy drive versus being on Instagram for 20 minutes, I could really tell the difference. After an outside adventure, I would come back with solutions and ideas and excitement. I'd be ready to dive back into my work or take that meeting with fresh enthusiasm.

After 20 minutes on Instagram? I'm tense and grumpy and anxious and usually wondering about all the things I am doing wrong rather than having inspired notions for what I can do next. The one exception is if I go on with a really clear intention. Like looking for inspiration for my own social posts or to get specific ideas for where to buy a product or how to do a workout.

Even then, I limit my time to about 5 minutes. Maybe 10. But the minute I struggle to breathe deeply or my shoulders get tense or Comparisonitis grabs hold of my thoughts, I close the app. I turn my attention to something beautiful like my apple tree, my puppy, or the sun sparkling in the noon sky.

Don't be tricked by the stimulus of social media or surfing. They're the energetic equivalent of sugar. It's really fun in small amounts on specific occasions. But looking to it as a regular source of nutrition is one hell of a roller coaster ride. And it will only deplete you and make you a cranky diabetic.

I give myself rules for my phone. When I can use it. How long I can use it. Checking if it's helping me complete a task or it's stealing time from what I truly want to be doing.

I use different questions to ask whether being on my phone is the best use of my attention. I have a list of questions that cut through my excuses and illuminate any feelings. They help me understand why I'm *really* grabbing my phone.

A few of these are:

~ Am I nervous about something and avoiding my feelings?

~ Am I bored and grabbing the easiest stimulus available?

~ Am I worried that I've missed out on something?

~ Am I anxious about getting a reply to a message?

~ Am I making bold moves and it's stirred up fear?

~ Am I looking for connection?

~ Do I need my phone to do this task?

~ Could I do this on my laptop?

~ Do I need a break right now?

You might have different reasons for grabbing your phone. Given how easy it is for us to hide in our devices these days, I encourage you to ask your own bold questions about why you've picked up your phone and is it going to deliver you joy?

If the answer is yes, like watching a hilarious video or receiving a little pebble love from a friend. Pebbling is the phenomenon of friends sending posts via Instagram as gestures of love — like wild penguins offering pebbles to a loved one as a gesture of care.

That might be just the lift to put you in a joy state that energizes your next creative burst. Another fun source of joy is to explore travelling a little farther afield. Stretching your courage to go outside the familiar to find exquisite downloads of delight.

I find there are, inevitably, times when I feel restless and bored with what is in easy reach. I can almost predict them with the seasons. I meant that literally! Autumn and spring are classic times when I feel like I need to stretch my legs, open my wings, and go further than my typical routes.

That's when I know I'm craving a bigger inflow of stimulus. Often, it feels like I am tired of seeing all the same places, faces, and stories. I need and want surprises and unexpected ideas. Conversations that feel different than the ones I'll hear within a 50km radius of my home.

Cultures that are curious to me, that bring me delight. That have different values and priorities than where I live. They stretch what I assume to be true and bring new ideas to my creative mind.

When I am frustrated by the "sameness" of what I see and feel and hear around me — that's when I know that the creative input that I need is travel.

Travel can mean going two hours from where you live. Or going all the way to Florence, Italy. It might mean finally attending that workshop or conference you've been longing for. Or visiting the town that inspired your latest creation. Travel takes time, energy, and money, but I also find it is one of the most generous sources of stimulation.

It gives back (at least!) what you invest in time, money, effort, and courage.

I make a point of going to New York City every year. It's my go-to place where I can drink in the sheer breadth of creative expression. Fashion. Architecture. Theatre. Cuisine. Conversation. Dancing. Music. You name it, New York has it!

I drink from the firehose of creativity when I'm in Manhattan. I rarely create while I am there. Instead, I charge my creative batteries. Soaking up the sheer variety and capacity for wild and colourful expression. Trusting that I will use all of that stored stimulation once I return. Taking it all in is an essential service and offering to my creative muse.

If going to a local café gives a slow (but steady) charge to my creative battery, then travel gets my charge to full. Once or twice a year, I need to get my battery topped up. Otherwise, I get restless and creatively frustrated. It's like I've been eating the same food, seeing the same people, hearing the same languages for *far* too long.

As creatives, we have a responsibility to stretch ourselves. To feel uncomfortable and bust our assumptions and try out new things. That may have different parameters for each of us, but if we're not partaking in this world, who are we creating for? How are we expanding our horizons and our potential as contributors?

Travel is one of the surest ways to rattle my comfort zone. It guarantees that I will talk with people I wouldn't have met. To challenge my brain to figure out a subway system or find a grocery store on a map or listen to a mind-blowing singer blast chills through my body with her solo on Broadway. That kind of stimulation has changed me forever and filled me with a quality of enthusiasm that reminds me what it means to be alive!

When was the last time you went somewhere new?

You can shake up your comfort zone by going to a new town nearby or a new country halfway around the world. For me, travel takes more energy than it did before the 2020 global pandemic. But the rewards are incredible.

The sheer confidence that comes from challenging yourself and the joy received by experiencing an event — like a concert, play, or conference — that just might change your life.

Even better? You get to bring those experiences back to your creative collaborators.

When you share your memories, you relive the delight and pass it on to them. Creating a beautiful domino effect of stimulation and inspiration! Making you a conscious conduit for bringing uplifting stimulation to your community.

How you choose to dialogue with stimulation depends on whether you're an introvert or extrovert. As an introvert, you may find listening to music and sketching with coloured pencils enough stimulation to rev up your creative engine. Or walking solo through the city streets and drinking in all the scenes without talking to anyone. Simply observing and enjoying.

For those of you who straddle the introvert and extrovert line (and I bet there are a lot of us who are a combination or alternate between the two), you may love the stimulation of a-synchronous conversations and brainstorming over apps like Voxer, Telegram, and WhatsApp. I've had many creative and business mastermind sessions over these tools, enough to spark me up and get me creating without even leaving my home.

Those apps give me access to creatives all over the world. Not just in my little corner of the planet. I want variety. I want diverse views. I want to be surrounded by creators who work in different mediums. It's kind of like having your own personal podcast episodes from people you love and adore. Episodes that are geared specifically to your challenges and wins.

The flow of creative energy works in person and over technology. So if you live somewhere that frustrates you because you haven't found your creative crew, connect over these apps. They saved my creative soul over the COVID years, and they continue to light me up today.

Whatever works best for you, make sure you include external and conversational stimulation as a key ingredient in your artist dates. Your productivity and creations will thank you for giving them the fuel that elevates what you create.

And the connection makes your journey a lot more fun!

Chapter Seven

Study

V ENTURING INTO THE WORLD gives me energy to create fresh and new projects. Diving into the work of others is the internal journey that kickstarts my ideas.

Learning from others is one of the greatest joys of being creative. There were times when I found this intimidating. But as I grew in confidence and understood that there is MORE than enough room for everyone's genius, I found it inspiring.

If someone created a masterpiece that you aspire to — amazing! This is a beautiful gift that illuminates so many questions and possibilities.

When you get curious about what you admire, you get clear on what matters to you. Explore and examine what you love about their accomplishment. If it provokes feelings of competition — great! Lean into those and feel everything that you need to feel. Those emotions are showing you what you desire. And the impact you want to make.

Once the waves of envy or anger or awe (or whatever else comes up) pass, dive into what inspired you. This is when I like to ask ALL the questions. Anything and everything that you want to know about why this work provoked you — intellectually, emotionally, physically, spiritually. Great work rattles and inspires us on multiple levels. Be sure to explore them ALL.

I take those questions to my journal first. I dive deep and explore what I loved, envied, questioned, and what the work provoked in me. What did you feel as the audience? Before you noticed the craft. Start with what it lit up in your soul. Before jumping to your desire as a creator.

When I do that, I often discover even more questions and emotions than what showed up on the surface. Every question is a goldmine for understanding what you love, care about, hate, want, imagine, and dream.

I ask questions like:

~ What made it work so well?

~ What did I love about the structure or rhythm?

~ What made it fresh and unique?

~ What feelings did it spark in me?

~ What do I admire about it?

~ How did this creator shake up my expectations?

~ What got me excited or offended?

I use these questions as a jumping-off point to dive into why this work (book, movie, event, fashion spread, whatever it was) got me so lit up that I want to make my version. When I study a brilliant or original work in the medium where I create, I consider that a portal to knowing what really matters to me.

I experienced this very feeling when *Big Magic* by Elizabeth Gilbert came out.

I had recently left the film industry and was only a few years into writing novels. So much of what she wrote in that book resonated with me. In fact, it resonated deeply enough that there was a *tiny* part of me that wished I had written it.

But of course, NO ONE except Liz Gilbert was meant to write *Big Magic*. That's what made it so magical.

Side note: Liz Gilbert has shared that many women came up to her when she was on tour with this book and accused her (yes ~ *actually* accused her) of writing *their* book. Mind-boggling, really. Her response was (and I am paraphrasing): *I wrote this one. Go write yours.*

By contrast, I knew that what I loved about *Big Magic* was that Elizabeth Gilbert captured the magic and spirit of creating and gave me the enormous gift of saying it out loud. I felt seen and understood. Two of the most powerful impacts that a book can have.

I felt emboldened and inspired by her book. I am forever grateful. In fact, I re-read *Big Magic* at least every two years. It's become one of my creative touchstones.

I never thought I'd have written *Big Magic*. It wasn't even remotely like a book I would write. It is beautiful, elegant, and hilarious — and so very Elizabeth Gilbert. The point that I took away and I hope others did, too, is that *I saw myself in those pages*.

So many books – especially by men – approach creativity from an incredibly tangible and schedule-oriented approach. How to shoehorn your way through the creative process. When so many women feel the magic and the gift of dancing with creativity. There is something otherworldly and logic-defying about this whole endeavour.

And, in many ways, it's the feeling of that magic that makes it all worthwhile. Like by touching that spark, we remember what it was like to be a five-year-old filled with wonder and belief and dreams that lit us up for days.

Every time I return to *Big Magic*, I am a different creator. I take something new from its pages. Some new pearl of wisdom is the one that sets off a chain reaction. I have a collection of books, movies, TV shows, songs, and creative folks that I go to when I need to reignite my creative energy and spirit. When I need inspiration or to invigorate my faith.

I recommend creating your own favourites collection. The ones that nurture your faith, speak to your heart, make you laugh, inspire you to be just a little bit crazier (or bolder), that restore your belief in your dreams, or make you love what you do a little deeper. These are precious gifts that move us forward. And remind us that we came here to love our work and be lit up by the work of others.

And learning from others is one of the greatest ways to feel inspired and rejuvenated.

***

The beginning of my career as a screenwriter was one of the most wildly magical experiences in my life. On what seemed like a whim, a friend invited me to attend a weekend workshop in Vancouver on the Art and Craft of Screenwriting.

"Screenwriting?" I thought. "What the heck is that?" It sounds hilarious to me now, but at the time, I had absolutely *no* idea that movies were made from scripts that individual writers made.

I was instantly hooked.

That weekend opened a door into a whole other world. I dove headfirst into the deep end. I wanted to know everything there was to learn about screenwriting. I read everything about the craft of writing, story, and film. And I found writer friends whose appetite for learning was as voracious!

We sought out the best stories that had made their way to film or television, dissecting what made them work and why. We were consumed with understanding the mechanics of story, character, emotion, pace, structure, and creating an effect that moved people.

I look back on that time with admiration. Somewhere inside my heart, I knew that studying the brilliant craftspeople who had come before me was the yellow brick road to understanding. I read many books and went to multiple workshops and conferences.

Yet, it was the practical studying of scripts, movies, and TV shows where I collected the evidence I needed. Proof that weaving a powerful story was the foundation for an incredible and lasting work of art. I felt like the creative writers (actors, directors, editors, and more) were whispering their secrets to me. Showing me what was possible when I paid close attention.

I felt close to those creators. That whatever they achieved was possible for me, too. And in studying their work, I was a part of a community, a history. I naturally experienced a camaraderie that is a gift of being creative.

Much like Elizabeth Gilbert pointed out that we don't need to carry a psychic burden of believing that we are the source of the creative genius that flows through us. I also believe that we are a thread in a tapestry of creative endeavours. We don't make our offerings in isolation of the genius that came before us, or is happening around us. We are part of weaving the universe.

Why would we want to stand as the solitary explorer on top of the mountain? To me, that feels cold and lonely. Never mind that no one ever climbs a mountain without help. It's a fallacy of the rugged individualist age. Everyone learns from each other - and if you resist that idea, it's worth asking yourself why?

Studying the genius and craft of others can accelerate and elevate your creations. Beyond that, I believe that we're designed to collaborate. And be a part of a greater creation. Just as we are re-discovering that we are part of nature and the earth. We creatives are remembering that this path is so much more rewarding and fun when we are connected.

I love that diving into the work of my predecessors feels like they are gifting me their guidance. That by exploring what they did well, and what they fumbled, I get to decide what works for me. Where I fit in the creative tapestry of making my life and this world.

I also love to see what others do that I don't need to accomplish. What a relief! I receive wisdom, stories, and ideas while knowing that I've been relieved of that project. Another creative person took care of it.

The more I get to know my gifts, the better it feels to let go of all the niches and corners that aren't mine to own. If this notion feels foreign to you, it's not a coincidence. Artists and creatives have been told for centuries that we must compete with one another to survive. A cornerstone of the poverty mindset is that we have to knock aside the others in our lane.

I am not denying that surviving and thriving as a creative entrepreneur is challenging. It takes immense courage and trust to endeavour to make the world while making a living. And still. A huge shift for me in my joyful state (and a lot less panic and burnout) came when I realized that I was meant to deliver on what I do well and what I am excited to do.

When I approached my path like everyone was a competitor and I had to snatch up whatever crumbs I could — was exactly what kept the old oppressive system in place. As I let go of *what was never meant* to be mine, I attracted more generous artists.

Slowly, I found myself surrounded by generous people. People who also believed there were more than enough projects to go around. And more than enough opportunities.

That shift brought me back to the joy of studying and appreciating the genius of others. I could read a book without feeling like I needed to compete with how that writer structured the plot or wove her characters. I could watch a TV show and revel in the brilliant delivery. I could appreciate the workshops where someone knew a LOT more than I did on that subject matter.

I was free to drink it all in. Receive it. To learn and choose what elevated my work. I felt part of a collaborative community — which was always part of my dream.

When I discovered the wild world of screenwriting, I was excited that a career existed where I could make money from making stories in an inherently collaborative medium. Being surrounded by creatives who all had a specific set of skills and gifts was heaven.

I was in awe of the actors who delivered emotion with such vulnerability. I was grateful for editors who would restructure a plot point for stronger impact. I was delighted by costume designers and sound engineers whose talents boggled my senses.

The more I embraced the creative wave that flowed from the creative gods and goddesses around me, the more lit up I felt by what was possible. This is the deepest gift of study. Whether from books, podcasts, plays, or travel, study busts through limited thinking and blows open the idea boxes in your brain.

I believe that study is a key part of a growth mindset. The minute that I decide that I have nothing more to learn on a subject, I feel the atrophy and cynicism taking hold.

Why not approach your craft and business with curiosity and wonder? It's so much more fun!

***

Learning and questioning provide a rich flow of energy and provocation.

Exploring and learning new skills is one of my greatest joys in life. It's how I challenge myself. How I feel young. How I know I am truly alive and excited to experience a new day.

Learning is expansion to me. And expansion is vitality. When I lose interest in learning anything, I know that I am full from absorbing information or I am burnt out. Either way, that's my red flag to take a break. But most mornings, I bounce awake keen to try something new.

Whether you vibe more with experimenting or learning, both are delightful ways to feel alive. I know that if I push myself a little, I'm expanding my skill-set and my mindset. I'm most excited when exploring skills that further my creative exploits.

Sure, I love to learn a new jump rope move or historical fact, but the truth is that I am way more excited by those tidbits if they are going to pay dividends in something I create. A story, a talk, a meditation, or a social post.

One quick exception: when you're deeply depleted from adulting or from work, then replenishing is a beautiful way to light the fire in your heart. I've had years when I stretched myself a LOT. So, by the time I reached December, I had little interest in anything new for my business.

But learning something for the pure joy of it? That put a smile on my face! Even if I have no idea why a mixology class or a wreath-building workshop makes my heart happy, I can rest easy knowing that anything that lights up my heart is the best choice for my creative soul.

Take a moment to think about how learning and studying support your day.

Maybe it's trying a new prompt for AI or exploring a new piece of software. Maybe it's expanding your notion of community and building connection with people who live in different countries. Maybe it's researching fashion from the 1920s while developing backstories for your characters in a story.

I believe that exploring is the lifeblood of creatives. As much as we are driven to make, we are also driven to discover. If I have to create the same thing over and over like a machine? I lose interest, and my energy drops quickly.

If I get to discover while making and, even better, scare myself a little in the process? Well, hell's bells, I am over the moon ready for that adventure! (Yes, I have been watching a lot of *Ted Lasso* episodes!)

Every time I brainstorm, write, or speak, I find something out about myself. It's usually hidden until I am deep in the creative process. After, I realize what in me has changed. What I uncovered... and it points the way to what I am excited to learn next.

For some creatives, learning got scarred during their school years. I was blessed with some amazing teachers who taught me to think critically and ask questions. I also had awful teachers who belittled me when I was curious. Some of those teachers were stuck in the archaic notion that women couldn't be the top of their class.

If school felt like a chore or a prison, studying might rub some of you the wrong way. Especially if studying brings back memories of parents being harsh or teachers being judgmental.

When anything feels heavy or angry, grab a journal or a voice note app and explore your *definition* of studying. Throw out any ideas you got in school. Give yourself full permission to change it to whatever lights up your heart.

And if you still love studying despite those experiences? You deserve a full-blown tickertape parade!

I want studying to equal exploration and/or deepening your craft. Learning from others who are a little (or a lot) ahead of you. Following your curiosity about how something works. Wondering why you got so revved up watching an episode of The Diplomat or teared up during the finale of The Great British Bake Off.

When you get curious or enthusiastic, it's a sparkling clue that your heart wants to follow. Fan that flame. Lean into wonder. Trust your curiosity. The more you give it rein to run, the further it will carry you. And trust your variety of studying. It looks different for everyone.

For my partner, it's diving down YouTube rabbit holes every time he picks up the TV remote. Or throwing himself into the craziest adventure he can dream up like solo camping in Botswana or scuba diving in Thailand.

For me, it's devouring about 10 books at once — fiction and non-fiction. Travelling to new places to hear different languages and watch people. To wander streets that I've never walked. And figuring out a new software program that can make my creative work easier and more fun. Plus, having delightful and fiery conversations with my creative besties.

What I need in the learning realm changes from month to month, season to season.

There are times when I dive into travelling and soak up the learning in person. That's when I study a new culture, language, way of living, the sensory delights, the rich imaginative sparks as I walk the streets. I get to lean into a fresh way of living and see what I want to take home with me. And potentially weave it into a story, course, or podcast.

At other times, especially in autumn, I dive deep into novels and television shows. Learning through my imagination while paying close attention to the brilliance in the craft. Fiction feels like virtual travel to me, as well as a chance to explore another person's experiences. It's a relief to hang out in someone else's world for a while. And it stretches my perception of what's possible.

The most important element of study is, of course, that you are learning something. But it doesn't have to be a big, new lesson. You might watch a film for the twelfth time, and have a fresh realisation. Or you notice an emotional choice on a deeper level.

You might go on a walk you've taken one hundred times before, only to see it from a new perspective in the wintertime. You might travel back to where you grew up, and it's a completely different place. Or you see it through very different eyes fifteen years later. You might meet back up with someone that you knew as a teenager only to discover that life is a wild ride and she shows up in a way that connects with you.

All these experiences provoke questions and curiosity. I relate to places that I've travelled to many times differently depending on what my year has been like and what I need in that specific moment. I get curious about different areas or people or events, depending on what interests me or how I have changed in the past 6-12 months.

Sometimes I go to New York City hungry to see shows and talk to people and find the latest cool shop that has popped up in the West Village. And there have been trips when I kept to myself, hermitted in my hotel room, and frequented the same café over and over to journal and to learn by listening to the regulars.

Study comes as deeply from returning to your favourites as it does from finding the newest trend. They're like the much-loved friend who brings you new ideas and viewpoints every time you meet for coffee. The richest places and creations in your life deliver that kind of inspiration.

Have you experienced that feeling? Been in the grasp of somewhere or someone so profound that you intuitively knew that you'd be coming back over and over. Each time taking a new shiny jewel from their treasure trove? I know chefs who feel that way about Julia Child's cookbooks. And actors who feel that way about interviews on *Inside the Actor's Studio.*

Finding these gems is a gift of being curious and creative. You know there is no competition. That in finding these beautiful creations, you're given a lighthouse on your journey. An offering that will give you inspiration and revelation each time you pick it up.

Take some time to explore what or who your favourite teachers are. Is it a particular book? A wonderful elder? A country or coast that illuminates something inside your heart each time you visit? The sound of a specific language? Listening to Glenn Gould play Bach on the piano?

Many of the treasures that you list won't be in your creative arena. I encourage you to make one list that is (for me, it would be storytellers, speakers, podcasters, writers, and thought leaders) and make another list that is all about expanding your horizons. Whether that inspiration is emotional, sensual, spiritual, cultural, intellectual - you get to fill that list with anyone or anywhere that lights you up. That gives you a beautiful feeling of challenge and expansion.

If study is meant to give us anything? It's delight and expansion.

Once you have that list, I want you to make a note to visit one of your favourites every week. You don't have to stay long. You could just crack open a book and read three pages. You could listen to ten minutes of a podcast. Or bask in the sound of someone's voice.

Treat your study time like a precious offering. A chance to connect with the creative treasures that replenish your heart, spark your curiosity. And keep you far away from the barren land of cynicism and rigid thinking.

As adults, we're too often told to take a stand and be an authority. And yes, to be sure, that's such a gift. To know and love something so well that we are the expert in our field. That we get to share that with others is an incredible feeling!

I want to advocate that study is an opportunity to return to, as the Buddhists call it: *beginner's mind*. To remember the relief found in not knowing everything. That, really, we know a tiny speck in the grand universe of knowledge and understanding.

I don't know about you, but for me, that is a BIG relief!

I want to feel curious and excited and full of wonder until the day I shuffle off this mortal coil. I want to know that each day, I can lean back into the arms of discovery. To learn from my predecessors while carving my brave, creative path.

By balancing between bold creations and humble learning, I get to be a beautifully whole person. Never assuming that I know too much, while claiming and celebrating what I do know.

In the centre of that little Venn diagram, is the sweet spot of being a joyful creative.

***

Study is an act of receiving. As creatives, we put so much energy out into the world. It's how we're designed and a huge part of why we are here. And inflow is equally important.

There are days when I don't want to share my thoughts or broadcast an idea. When I am in a quieter, more introverted mood. When my heart and soul need the wise words of another. Or a cosy story that carries me to another town. Reminding me of the pure joy of fun and discovery.

My version of study is unique to who *you* are and what *you* need. It's that quiet (or ecstatic!) nourishment that comes with knowledge...questions... and feeling provoked by another person's gift to the world.

Let's grab back that word — study — and make it ours!

Study can be staring up at the night sky. Laying back on a surfboard to study the sound of the ocean. It might be what Timothy Findley did when he was writing *Not Wanted on the Voyage*. He crawled on a beach on his hands and knees (impervious to the judgmental gazes of others) to understand the perspective of his narrator. Who, *spoiler alert*, is a cat.

Study is the thrill of exploration. The adventure of ideas. The wild expanse of the universe. It's trusting that you have a sharp mind and an open heart and are wired for the pursuit of wisdom. It's about blowing apart your assumptions rather than shoring them up. And rediscovering the fierce-eyed nosiness of a child.

Let's expand Study to include soaking up insights that fuel you to go far with a heart full of joy. I imagine dancers study so many of their predecessors and peers. Watching a wide range of styles and moves, from ballet to street battles. They might even study the swift elevation of a hummingbird and the graceful flight of a great blue heron.

Why limit yourself? Why not follow the intuitive needs of your soul? To uncover the creative and imaginative sparks that you know will give you what you need.

Challenge any assumptions that threaten to calcify your mind. We're here to deepen, expand, connect, and collaborate. That requires stretching and challenging yourself. Especially when you're feeling most entrenched.

When I'm feeling especially defensive or aggravated, it's a sign that I need to let go. To breathe.

I need to remember that creating comes faster and easier when I'm not "gripping the handlebars" — as we say in the cycling world. When you are riding up a hill or chasing a faster cyclist, you have a natural tendency to clench the handlebars. It's reflexive — and it's a waste of energy. So you learn to catch the habit and release the grip. To lighten your touch.

One dear friend who taught me about cycling over long distances called it "piano hands." Play lightly with your fingers on the handlebars so that your body is relaxed. And you ride with grace. You save at least thirty percent of your energy. And when you're riding 100, 120, or 160km? That makes a big difference!

When you're in the middle of a six-month writing project, a two-month programme development schedule, a three-month podcast tour, or the tail-end of a 12-month business adventure, you're going to need piano hands as a mantra.

Take a moment to imagine it ~ lighten your grip, trust your direction, play lightly with your effort ~ you'll notice that a deep breath and relaxed body come naturally. Piano hands is kind to your nervous system, your overall energy, and your team.

Study is a beautiful application of piano hands.

Loosening my grip on being the only expert in the room or in my niche. It reminds me that there is an abundance of support. The world is full of brilliant people offering creative magic. Learning is a loving act of appreciation. When we reach for the genius of others.

The universe has many ways of expanding you. Supporting you. And showing you new insights.

I guarantee you'll be surprised, amazed, and best of all, replenished. You'll find new forms of art. Discover fresh places to visit. Make new friends (whether they're alive or centuries old). Get schooled by ancient philosophers and modern musicians.

You'll rediscover a beautiful smile on your face. Like I do, when I feel the delight of a realisation and the light-hearted sensation of being held by many creative souls.

When I feel deep appreciation, rather than envy, I'm hanging out in the realm of professional creatives. That is pure receptivity and joy.

And it's the bridge to the initiation of creative sparks.

Chapter Eight

Sparks

W HEN I GIVE MYSELF time to study and replenish, that's when the creative sparks fly.

This may seem like a normal, everyday experience of being creative. But once you've been doing this for a while, you inevitably find yourself in a creative drought. It might last only a day or a week. It might last a month. But it will happen.

A drought comes along when you drained your well and forgot to refill it. It's the result of pushing to keep up with the "you must produce 24/7" culture. Droughts can also happen when you've just finished a stressful time — one that demanded a lot of energy.

I used to think they only came from overwork or crossing a project finish line. But I've discovered that they also happen after a season of giving away a lot of energy. That might happen by taking care of someone for a long period, or the world being thrown into a pandemic, or an excessively combative federal election.

If I'm not conscious of where I spend my energy and attention, it flows to people and situations that I have ZERO control over. This is the greatest waste of my vitality. It's wildly easy to give away my creative attention to situations that I can't change. Of course, it's natural to feel and integrate any emotions about the situation. That's healthy.

After that? I want to put my energy where I have impact. Otherwise, I end up drained and defeated.

The most recent time this happened was during the U.S. 2024 election cycle. A country that I don't even live in! I have dear friends in the U.S. My energy spent supporting and encouraging them was well worth it.

My energy getting upset about the politics and lack of civility between human beings? This may have been important for me to process and recognize — especially as a caring person who knows we are all connected. But after the initial upset, continuing to let the news wind up was a complete waste of time and energy.

I had no influence over those ranting heads on television. They weren't even my representatives.

After the election, I took a long stretch of time to reflect. I retreated from the world. I asked myself a lot of questions. And I recognized how little creative energy was in my tank.

It felt like every other creative drought that I'd experienced — after completing a novel or delivering a project or getting through a crazy season of house renovations.

I was understandably frustrated! I had given away my precious creativity to something that resulted in nothing of value.

So, I took that oh-so-important step back. I followed my recipe of tending to my soul. I used my go-to activities, as well as treasured alone time. This is why I want you to have a go-to list. The list of practices that tend to your heart — and hold true to them *no matter what anyone else thinks you need*.

I'll admit that I *still panic* when I find myself in a creative drought. Even though I've walked this territory more often than I can say. Each time, it comes with an uneasy sense of dread that I will never feel the spark again. Or I may get tiny sparks, but they won't be strong enough to kindle a fire that lasts.

If you're in this phase, consider this your reminder that you're human. You need to tend to your heart to feel the flow of inspiration. And to feel the desire to do anything with that inspiration.

This is self-care for creatives. We've come a long way in accepting self-care, but we still have a long way to go. Taking good care of yourself is the key to creating from a place of joy, rather than panic, anxiety, or a need to prove yourself.

When I find myself in a creative drought, I know it's an important sign. It's my creativity's way of telling me to tend my joy.

Sparks need light and oxygen. When the world or a project has compressed me into a tight, crushed ball, there is no way that any air or heat is getting through until I allow myself to breathe.

If you take good care of your creative energy, the spark *always* comes back. That's why the most important thing you can do is keep a kind eye on your spark. It's natural to forget, to get obsessed, to be determined to push something to the end.

I've done all those things. It's incredibly easy to do when I get whirled into the cultural pace of push-push-push, struggle-shove-hustle. Which works for a while and inevitably brings me back to exhaustion.

The worst part about exhaustion? It sucks away my joy, and messes with my head. The times when I am most susceptible to doubt and despair are when I have ground myself into a little pile of overworked dust. The more often I do that, the more convinced I can get that it HAS to be part of the creative process. Except I absolutely, unequivocally know that it doesn't.

Here are a few LIES I am determined to debunk:

~ Burnout is an inevitable part of being a life-long creator.

~ You must hustle to prove you are worthy.

~ There's only *one* way to be committed as a creative — daily with NO breaks.

The more I pay attention to my spark and put its vitality first, the easier it is to create and feel great doing it. That means adding breaks. And being brave enough to do the work MY way. What works for me doesn't need to match my peers, my mentors, or my friends. It just needs to be what makes my creativity happy.

Being firm in your way can feel uncomfortable at first.

~ Does it mean you need to be aware? *Yes.*

~ Does it mean you need to have courage? *Yes.*

~ Does it mean you'll need to ignore disbelievers? *Heck yeah.*

~ Does it mean you're a brave soul who cares for herself? *It does!*

Choosing your way means that every time you start a new project, you know yourself a little better. You'll start from that place and explore deeper. And you'll be dancing your special path.

***

These days when I come through a creative dry spell, I reframe it as a fallow time. When I need to allow my inspiration to rest. And still, each time my spark returns, I am relieved and over-the-moon grateful.

When the rhythm of joy comes back, it feels like I'm coming back to life. That my energy has filled past the E (for empty) in my tank. And I need to get to a quarter tank full before I consider building anything with my energy.

When the ideas start flowing, I'm thrilled! Every spark is precious. Each one is my creativity whispering. Letting me know that it's still here. Sharing secrets, capturing magic, suggesting clandestine meetings in the middle of the night.

I feel like a child again. Full of wonder. Craving adventure. Thrilled by the rush of imagining a new bonfire, a wild adventure, a delightful new trail to explore. At this stage, these wild and unpredictable sparks disappear almost as quickly as they appear. Much like the first few strikes and blows of making a fire in a damp forest.

But when I keep blowing on those initial sparks (with stimulation, study, and inspiration), I invariably find the captivating project that propels me back into creative momentum. And when the sparks show up steadily, I no longer feel constricted or braced.

My faith returns. And I'm ready to welcome the curiosity that comes with sparks evolving into bigger ideas. And at this tender point, it's important not to rush. The relief of creative ideas flooding in can ignite the panic that I need to do something with them — as soon as possible — to prove I can still make things. That all is not lost!

Yes, it really does feel that dramatic.

If you have also felt the panic of a season without a project, the first flush of ideas isn't the time to commit (*yet*). This is when you revel in the joy of being creative. Letting the wonder, delight, and novelty of multiple ideas thrill your soul.

Panic wants you to pounce on the first idea that comes along. It's still convinced that you won't get another shot at this, so grab what comes along. If you approached dating with the same theory, you'd end up on a roller coaster of disappointment!

The first sparks are designed as signs that your creativity has returned to the playground. Your engines are firing. They're meant to give you faith that all is well, and you'll know when an idea capable of going the distance comes along. The best kind of magical partnership.

I'm the kind of creative that loves having at least one (usually more like three or four) creative projects going at one time. So when the inevitable and necessary quiet times come, I can feel lost. Like something is missing. I remind myself that resting when climbing a mountain is just as important as striding forward.

I imagine that this message is counter to practically everything you've read or heard about being creative. Show up. Keep going. No matter whether you do anything. Keep the habit. And yes, I do agree with all of that.

Except — a key difference in the joyful creating method is that inspiration, exploration, brainstorming, and collaborative conversations are vital parts of the creative process. Along with rest. They aren't being lazy or avoidant. When you rest mindfully, it's an essential stage of allowing ideas and inspiration to come to you.

Like the earth, we need to rest. Winter gives the trees and the soil and the animals a chance to hibernate. We're not designed to go forward at full speed all the time. Winter isn't without activity. A lot is going on. And our rest times during creative endeavours is the same. So much is going on under the surface and in our extended reality. You're listening and gathering and integrating. You're preparing for the next rush.

After resting, when you feel those first sparks, it's like the time before Spring. When the sap begins to rise from the tree roots and the world beneath the ground is waking up. Those sparks bring a whoosh of springlike energy that herald the return of creative curiosity.

I ADORE this feeling. It's one of my favourite sensations. Ideas are bubbling inside, and your soul is dialoguing with inspiration. Assessing whether this is a little or big idea.

Does it tip the row of dominos that lead to a bigger idea? Or does it have a bigger purpose all on its own?

Sometimes a curious notion leads you to a café, that shows you a poster, that leads you to a concert, that connects you with a person, who introduces you to a band, and the creative spark is building.

So many ripples happen before your soul finds the project that it knows will sustain you for weeks, months, even years. During that exploration, your heart gets a sense of whether this is the right match. Much like with a person or a career or a home.

Creative projects are not merely past times. They're not just an activity that we're good at or that we've practised. They are a calling from your soul.

An invitation to play and explore and stretch in a way that evolves you as a person. A calling strong enough that you carry the light through stretches of darkness and, through the journey, you become a different person. A braver, more vulnerable person. A person who knows herself in a deeper, clearer way than when the journey began.

Finding that kind of soul-defining project takes time. Most ideas don't have the stamina (or I don't have enough interest in them) to cross the finish line. They're fun or a quick dalliance, but they don't compel you enough to get through the inevitable messy middle.

The first part of every project is intriguing. But like every relationship, once you get past the shiny initial exchange, you meet the stage when you have to decide whether you'll do the deeper work. When you need to believe *enough* in what you're doing that you keep going - even when you feel blind, tired, or lost.

The commitment required to carry a project to the finish line is *exactly* why I also believe in revelling in the first sparks. Regardless of whether the sparks lead to anything more than playful notions and the thrill of imagination.

Let yourself feel the *rush*. Be flirty! Play with each one. Treat it like idea dating. Take your notion out for lunch or a drive by the beach. Dress up for your creative dates. Explore new activities with your ideas. Just don't make any long-term promises (yet).

Too often, I've been desperate to find that right project. To grab a creative endeavour so I don't have to feel the discomfort of being in the "in between." It's awkward and frustrating to have people ask you, "What are you working on? What's next?" when you know you're in the desert. Waiting for the star that will lead you back to a magical path.

My word! I even did it in that last sentence! Why does the in-between time need to be a desert?

Yes, it's a stage that can feel strange because I'm flirting with ideas rather than getting down to the business of producing something of substance. But every stage of creating is a sacred part of the path. Fighting any phase is denying the power this one is meant to give you.

The *thrill* of the sparks stage is that it cultivates your creative energy. It's an opportunity to play and deepen trust in your intuition. It's respecting that not every project deserves your undivided devotion. And, therefore, it makes sense that you take some time to figure that out. It alleviates the pressure of delivering and prioritizes imagination as its own reward.

Dr. Christiane Northrup, board-certified OB Gyn, author and speaker, compared birthing books to birthing babies. She shared that both involve bringing forth new life, as a child or a creative endeavour. And if you believe that any long-term creative project is going to require that level of transformation, you deserve to give yourself time to find the one you truly believe in.

The rush to be productive (or to avoid looking lazy) can override your intuitive knowing. Our minds love to spin all kinds of tales when we're not moving forward with something that keeps them entertained. Even when you choose the soul-enlivening project, you will bump into a stage when everything else looks MUCH shinier. Especially when you're stuck in the messy middle.

THIS is why choosing the one you believe in matters. Because when those inevitable moments of temptation appear, that's when your original commitment requires recommitment. You choose that love and desire over and over throughout your endeavour.

You rekindle the spark that started your project over and over again. To climb the wild, windy mountain to completion.

***

If commitment brings steadiness, the spark phase brings adventure!

One of my tried-and-true methods to ignite creative sparks is the brilliance of other creatives. Whether listening to a podcast, watching a YouTube video, or indulging in a beloved TV series, I often receive intuitive nudges and idea ignition.

Suddenly, one phrase or inspired exchange ignites a spark that leads to a series of questions and curious explorations. It's a thrilling moment when I shift from not feeling inspired, to being lit up inside. Like someone strikes a match and, once again, I'm fully alive.

So how do you cultivate sparks? Start with your sources of sparks. What are the activities, people, conversations, and places that deliver intuitive ideas to you? Make a list. And don't concern yourself with whether it matches anyone else's. Your creative sourcing is meant to look and feel unique to you.

Once I've received ideas through my creative go-tos, I will feed that spark. Sometimes that means finding more conversations about the topic. Exploring books, podcasts, and videos. Going after the spark to see if it's going to last beyond a brief shot of light. All the while remembering the intention of revelling in the energy, rather than building anything.

If this ignition came from being around other enthusiastic creatives, I brainstorm and seek out ways to be in that company. Find that energy. See where it leads. That might mean a trip to the city, setting up regular creative dates with friends, or finding a series of talks that I can attend.

I'll do my best to find the most accessible options. That way, this phase doesn't require complicated or expensive endeavours. But if it's been a while? And I know in my heart that going to a creative place like NYC or Edinburgh would fire me up? Then I do it.

Much like Joy Dates, cultivating sparks is both a weekly endeavour *and* a specific creative phase. The in-between projects stage is an essential time to revel in creative sources that fuel you. To receive from other makers. And allow a connection to the universal creative tapestry to inspire you.

Another of my go-to ways of getting sparked is to have passionate conversations with other creatives. We can talk about art, politics, spirituality, goals, astrology, gardening, psychology, and so much more. I feel the delight of the conversation while simultaneously noticing which ideas spark more questions. And which notions that I've already grown bored of.

Both are powerful clues to what I want to pursue. And what currently fans my creative fire.

When I am exploring an idea that excites me, I'm choosy about who I share it with. My closest creative friends and companions understand if I tell them I am exploring without knowing where the path may lead. They get that sometimes I need to wander to collect the gems that will be integrated into my understanding or my future endeavours.

When the sparks start to lead to potential paths, I keep a lot of the discoveries to myself. Mostly so I am conscientiously fuelling my own fire. Instead of talking the spark out before it has a chance to build inner momentum.

This time is especially tender. People who are new to business or creative endeavours might take your curious exploration to be a declaration. Suddenly, the weight of other people's expectations can bog you down and keep you from staying light-hearted.

As hard as it is to contain excitement, at the spark stage, it's worth it! Keep all that joy and thrill to yourself like it's a secret project. Stoke that fire and feel the heat. You get to keep an idea to yourself for as long as you wish.

It may sound secretive, but it's a powerful approach to cultivating energy. If I tell everyone about an idea too soon, the fire scatters. It's like I've let all the heat out - instead of kept in a tight space and blowing on it to grow.

I've 100% lost interest in ideas this way. After talking about it with too many people, I spent all the curiosity. And the spark just petered out. I wasn't interested anymore. I have a sneaking suspicion that I was testing whether *other* people were intrigued by it. Whether *their* eyes lit up when I shared.

Some of this comes from the "share everything as soon as it happens" pressure of social media. Some of it comes from not trusting my own intuition about a project. And some of it came from needing other people's approval and enthusiasm

Even if you're not a regular on social media, the sheer excitement of having a creative spark can initiate the magnetic pull to tell the world about it. I implore you - *don't!*

Keep that secret for yourself. Enjoy it. Savour it. Trust that you're meant to get personal time with this relationship before it ever makes it into the world. It's kind of like enjoying dating someone before letting anyone know. Getting your own private cocoon time without the judging or curious questions of Aunt Matilda.

I tell my closest, most trusted confidants. The ones who understand my need to cherish this time. Maybe I even tell them if it's a book or a course or a business idea. But I won't give a lot of details.

This is the practice of creative boundaries. Protecting your little creative seedling. Like every other kind of boundary, it's the fastest way to see who supports you. And who doesn't respect your requests. That pushy or disrespectful group? They don't find out anything until I am deep into a project. When I am committed and unswayable.

Another upside to keeping your creative crush close to your heart is that you won't look for other people's approval or understanding. Neither of those are relevant. Not while you're tending to your own flame. And never until you decide you want someone's trusted and specific input.

I also encourage creatives to keep their ideas close so they remember that this is their romantic time. We become so serious as adults that we forget the joy of playing. Toying with ideas brings us so much delight and tests out how we feel. We may need to dance around the floor a few times before we discover that a series concept or a business idea matches our desire.

Other people's opinions can muddle your intuition and hijack your joy. No one else knows what is best for your creative mojo and your soul. That is between you and your intuitive knowing. They can't possibly understand why this project is either perfect for you or the wrong path.

And the moment other people weigh in? It can destroy the delicate seedling you've planted.

Rachel Hollis talks about this a lot – and uses the acronym, OPO (Other People's Opinions). She shares about it on *The Rachel Hollis Podcast* as well as in her book, *Girl, Wash Your Face*. She even has a hilarious flowchart that addresses what to do when someone has an opinion and either voices it or doesn't. In a nutshell, the outcome is always, "Don't worry about it!"

There are times when we need and want other people's input. And the spark phase is not that time. This is a creative stage that is ALL about you. It's your sandbox. Your playground. And your intimate time with the Divine and your creative joy.

No one else is needed during this party. Other than to add to your delight, energy, and expression. I highly recommend that you keep your nascent ideas close to your heart. When you feel the pull for someone else's approval (which is likely to happen), acknowledge it by:

Having a conversation with that need. Explore what it is that you're craving. Is it excitement? Is it reassurance? Are you scared that this idea might rock your world? Imagine that you're talking to your friend or even a creative mentor (you don't have to know them in real life). You can get the intuitive support you need by activating your brilliant imagination.

Journal it out. My journal is a go-to when I am overflowing with positive or negative thoughts. When my emotional load has grown too high or I am panicking and seeking another's opinion. Not for their insights but to calm and encourage me. When I pour it out, usually in stream of consciousness, I feel like I have met with the best friend or therapist in the world.

Walk. Dance. Sing. Move. As the sparks grow, so does your energy. I tend to want to sing an idea from the rooftops once I feel this building of enthusiasm. Instead of sharing your idea, get your groove on! Play music, sing, dance, go for a run! Or grab your keys and go for a drive while singing and dancing. Revel in this energy and stoke that fire by physically moving!

As someone who sources a lot of energy and joy by being around the enthusiasm of others, I deeply understand the desire to share your sparkly excitement. It's such a natural desire! When you get excited about an idea, you want your creative friends (and family) to be excited, too. To share in your delight and vision.

I promise there is a time for sharing! But a new idea is like that tiny spark that you've blown to life in a campfire. It's precious and might go out with the slightest shift in temperature or wind.

What that spark wants is for YOU to blow on it. To tend to it. And talk to it. To encourage that nascent notion to grow stronger.

I've shared enough new ideas to know that the odds of that spark getting extinguished are high. The reason? *You're* not even convinced. Women are trained from early in our lives to want other people's validation. To crave outside opinions on our choices. To tell us that, not only is it a good idea, but it will go the distance.

It's time that *you* choose *you* as that wise source of knowing. Your inner sense of what's good and important matters most. Especially with creative ideas that you'll be carrying, creating, and championing. No one else's input matters more than yours.

Prioritising your opinion and belief is a powerful shift. Cradle that spark in your heart. Trust that it's giving you what you need. That you understand the connection and are brave enough to follow your curiosity without the added cheering of your friends.

The more you believe in your inner wisdom, your intuitive sense, the more confident you get. You'll delight in the feeling that you have a creative secret. A little fire in your heart that you're fanning. Blow that spark into a flame by doing research and finding communities and checking out others who are developing

And if it goes out? No one will be the wiser. You'll know that spark served its purpose on your journey.

I have creative collaborators that I trust to follow my instructions when I ask them to be only enthusiastic. They would listen and be thoughtful if I told them that I'm not ready for feedback. And still, I keep the spark phase all to myself.

The longer that I treasure an idea as mine, and mine alone, the closer I feel to it. The deeper the connection grows. The more anticipation I feel about the time when I will share it with friends. By then my little fire has a hot enough burn that I'm confident it will survive any frost, wind, or downpours.

Creative sparks are precious. I remind myself of that truth often. I use it as a mantra. Revelling in this special time together. I know some authors who keep ideas close to their heart, under a veil of secrecy, until they are close to complete. Because they don't want to be influenced by anyone until they feel ready for their input.

You are the captain of your creative ship. No one else gets to make those choices. Not me, not your spouse, not your most trusted friends.

Love your sparks. Whether they last or not.

Every spark has a magical purpose.

Chapter Nine

Kindle

A s a spark takes hold and conjures a flame, you've reached the Kindle stage.

This is when one idea pushes away the others. A singular character or topic or business becomes the dominant song in my head. It's a lot like when you discover a new singer and you become obsessed with their latest song. Playing it over and over. Learning the words. Dancing to the amazing melody.

Your spark goes beyond a notion and turns into a full-blown flame because it becomes your main squeeze. The project that grabs your attention enough that everything else pales.

Sometimes, this feeling is a rush and goes to a blaze in no time. And sometimes, the feeling is a persistent whisper. Nudging me every day to come back to the project, dive in deeper, go a little further. In this context, I see obsession as a powerful and positive force. The crossroads where momentum and determination meet and partner up.

I've had ideas grow slowly from gentle affinity to friendly flirting to dating regularly. They feel like a slow dance with a natural and easy pace. Then there have been other ideas that grabbed me unexpectedly, ignoring that I was in the middle of writing a different project altogether. And the interloper sure as hell did not care that I was already waist-deep in another project!

My ideas tend to be a slow, steady burn, rather that the intense bonfire. But I've definitely had ideas whisk me off my feet. Like a "meet cute" in a romantic comedy; going from spark to blaze in record time.

That's how the *Great Lands* series dove into my heart. The first book, *Messenger*, showed up as a single scene years before I wrote the book. At the time, I was consumed by screenwriting, and my genres were thriller and romantic comedy.

When this mysterious scene from a fantasy story appeared, I didn't know what to make of it. I was intrigued, but I was also determined to succeed in film. So, I shoved aside the captivating imagery and went back to my obsession with writing screenplays.

Nevermind that novels intimidated me. Despite writing screenplays and TV pitches for years, novels were a secret land full of wild rules and open structure. I continued to write scripts until I reached my breaking point with the industry's misogyny. I'd had enough of trying to pitch stories with strong female protagonists to producers who loved the stories but kept wanting to change the female protagonist to a guy.

Breaking points are amazing catalysts. They require courage and powerful decisions. Saying no to a script deal and leaving the film biz was exactly that. My bold leap that inspired the audacious move into novel writing. I was terrified and thrilled — the ideal combo for change.

I started writing a completely different novel. In truth, I'd forgotten all about the mysterious woman in the cloak. The one who had nudged me years before and had clearly been waiting patiently for me to get over my obsession with thrillers and move on to romantasy.

And while my heroine from *Messenger*, Gabriella, was willing to put up with my screenwriting, she was sure as heck *not* going to stand aside while I wrote some *other* novel. She clearly didn't see screenwriting as competition. She knew her story would be a trilogy — and one that would grab hold of my heart for several years.

But let some other book be my first novel? Not on your life!

That spark simmered under the surface for years. When suddenly, like a rogue wildfire, it pushed above ground and swept through my world. That, for the record, is not my typical experience. But it's one of my favourite memories, even if it threw me for a major loop.

My guess is these days I'm a lot more aware of my desires. I don't shove *anything* aside without asking a lot of questions. The biggest one being — is this the project my soul needs most right now? Regardless of inconvenience or ego or creative medium.

If I had ignored Gabriella (again), I'm not sure that she would have tried a third time. And my reward? The process of writing *Messenger* was a joy. I let Gabriella show me the way. I trusted the story that was flowing through me and the many years of structure and study that I'd dedicated to my craft during my years in the film business.

By kindling the spark that spoke loudest to my heart, I started a powerful journey of trusting my intuition. I also rediscovered the pure joy of creating. While I was writing, I led with joy and the sheer thrill of writing. Rather than worrying about which genre was hot and was I delivering the story trend of the hour.

Trust me. Hollywood can mess with your intuitive sense of what to write. When so many people tell you *their* opinion of what's hot and how to succeed. *Spoiler alert!* 99% of the time, they are dead wrong. They're just really good at asserting opinions based on the *last* movie that was successful.

From the moment I started writing *Messenger*, I knew this book would change my life. And it absolutely did.

Here are a few of the ways:

~ *I became a novelist.* A feat I had been terrified of for a decade.

~ *I rediscovered my creative magic.* Despite a decade of prioritizing what others thought.

~ *I revelled in Gabriella's adventure.* After years of being told to tone my protagonists down. Or change them into men (true story).

~ *I realized this was book one of three.* My first novel would lead me to write a trilogy.

So how do you know if your current spark is the one to kindle? Creative projects have many reasons to come into our lives. Like relationships, some are a flirtation, some are a rebound, and others are a long-term commitment.

When I start a project, I want to finish it. I play with all kinds of ideas. But with a bigger project, I'm built for commitment. So I've learned to let many ideas go. I trust that every creative spark serves its own purpose. Some are fun. Some lead me to more questions. And some are destined to change me forever.

You might be a *flirt and leave it* kind of gal. I admire that! Knowing how you develop ideas and keep the fire alive is vital to a long-term, joyful relationship with your creativity. I believe in trusting your approach.

Understanding how you work. And knowing what keeps your heart's flame vibrant.

There are many kinds of creatives. I have some friends who are monogamous to a single medium. Whether that's film, TV, novels, or podcasts. They have a niche that they love and they go deep. They might be curious about other mediums, but they have zero interest in them beyond casual conversation.

If you're committed to your medium, you know what works. You understand what will light your heart up. You likely even have one genre or a specific structure. That gives a lot of clarity.

Trust your instincts about projects that fire up your curiosity. When a project intrigues you day after day? It will keep you going through the messy middle (where desire can stray).

I need to have at least two if not three, creative projects going at once. I used to feel weird and ashamed about it. Like somehow I wasn't as committed as my monogamous creative friends. That I lacked focus or interest. *Not true.*

When I have two projects that light me up, I switch off between them. By cultivating the fire of one, I get ideas for the other. And if they are different enough, they hone companion skills. I also swap when I get bored.

The hilarious part? It doesn't take long for me to miss the project that just 24 hours ago had me bored. Swapping between more than one keeps the flame alive — so my creative endeavours are happy. And so am I.

Right now, I have two wildly different companies I'm building. One is a food company, called *Flourish Kitchen*. It involves managing the cooking, freeze-drying, and promoting of low-allergen meals. It's a very physical and hands-on business.

The other is *Joyful Creating*. A largely digital product business that I create (mostly) on my own — with writing, speaking, and engagement. It's oriented to making and promoting books, courses, and an online community.

I've found that some folks find it easy to accept that I have these two creative projects. While others can't wrap their heads around it. This kind of back-and-forth stresses them out.

I've learned that it works for *me*. It keeps my flame burning — otherwise I get bored and feel trapped. When that happens? All momentum stops. I feel like I am trudging through mud.

As long as I check in with my body and maintain my healthy habits, I am lit up by this approach. I remind myself that everyone has a creative rhythm that works best for them.

By observing what works for you, you'll know how to kindle your own flame. Whether by dedicating yourself for a year to one project. Or bouncing back and forth between multiple projects. Or having a big, exciting life and getting up at the crack of dawn to forge your passion.

***

After years of creating – and planning to create for many more – I prioritize my wellbeing over my current venture. I balance my desire to take on a project with where I am in my life.

And I ask myself a bunch of questions:

~ What other commitments am I finishing?

~ Do I have enough fuel in my creative tank?

~ Will I get enough time with my family and loved ones?

~ What trips do I have planned this year?

~ How do I reach this goal and keep my joy flowing?

Being honest with myself is essential. As someone who can jump first and ask questions later with my creative enthusiasm, I've learned (the hard way) that asking questions *first* preserves my wellbeing, sanity, and momentum.

It's far too easy to jump in and find at the 25% mark that I wasn't *that* excited about the idea. Which has led to my being hard on myself for dropping things when I lose interest. A certain amount of experimenting is totally to be expected. And definitely encouraged!

But if you're someone who starts waaaay more projects than she finishes? It's important to interrupt any limiting patterns to find clarity *before* you commit. That clarity pays huge dividends in the long run. Not the least of which is feeling the exquisite joy of finishing a project and taking it out into the world.

After I enjoy the first date, ask my questions, and take a moment with my intuition — I trust my heart. She tells me when an idea has taken root. And that there's a way to reorient my calendar to make room for a project that lights me up.

I trust there's a divine timing that is unique to every project. Judging the current one by how the last book went or how quickly I created my last course is unfair and unhelpful. This soulful partnership has its own magic.

Listening to what the *project* needs and what *you* need is the recipe for joyful creating.

You are a sovereign creative. On your own journey. With your own brilliant way of doing things. Screw what you've seen on social media or sales pages or heard on YouTube.

Every project has its unique learning curve, potential, and pace. If the ups, downs, and critiques of social media have taught me anything, it's don't believe that there's *one way* to create, market, share, expand, or build a business.

Writing one book will differ from another. The liftoff of your latest business might look different if you have small children, when you didn't for your last one. Each creative fire has its own rhythm.

Plus, each time, you'll be at a different place in your life. Which means you'll have different priorities. And a different balance of time, energy, and money. The three essential ingredients to consider before leaping into a big project.

Sometimes, I have way more time than I have money. Other times, I'm struggling for energy and am okay for time and money. That might not determine whether I write the book or start the business, but it sure as hell *will* determine the pace.

So no matter what anyone else says — choose YOU first.

Your wellbeing is the most important ingredient - and taking care of it will pay off. Because the creative long game includes more than making your book, podcast, or art collection.

On the heels of making a beautiful thing, is sharing that creation with the world. A reality I ignored at my peril. I rarely factored in the creativity, energy, and love required for the promotion phase. That is a whole project of its own — and includes research, time, creating, and committing.

Taking the joyful creating approach will make sure you have energy and enthusiasm left to share about your miraculous creation. But I'm jumping way past the Kindle stage!

Let's get back to fanning that spark.

The Kindle phase doesn't require being farsighted or making a commitment (yet). I like to think of it as test driving ideas. Getting a feel for them. Reaping all the delight in getting to know it.

The more you play, the more you hone your intuitive sense of what feels right and what feels temporary. Play with as many ideas as you want! For as long as you want!

Just don't fall under the spell of constantly talking about ideas without finally choosing one. It can be very alluring to stay in the dating phase and not get down to the work of making.

The one exception is if you desperately need some creative playtime.

Maybe you're coming out of a phase of burnout or disillusionment. Or you're switching mediums and you're nervous about making your first pick. Like I was with novels! Or you're a workaholic, and you've never given yourself the chance to play with 15 ideas at once.

If one of those resonates, taking time to play is incredibly liberating. Letting go of being serious. Rediscovering your wonder. Getting curious about what you love. These are deeply healing phases that will mend your broken heart.

After I left the film industry, I grieved for almost a year. I had a strong sense that I wanted to write novels, but

I was heartbroken that my dream of being a produced screenwriter hadn't happened. I came so close. I had the LA agent, manager, and even a deal on the table. It was a huge leap of faith to leave, and it left me devastated and doubting myself.

For the first time, I was staring at the scariest question: *Do I want to write anymore?*

Way beyond anything else, *that* feeling terrified me. Who was I if I wasn't a writer? What would I possibly love as much as storytelling? What if I never felt excited to create again? Am I broken?

My heart aches for that past version of Kate. Deep in a dark night of the soul.

I found my way back by learning to play again. By taking my creativity back. By remembering that I create for ME first. For my joy. For my fun. For what I want to feel, explore, and offer. As a creative, my first commitment is to my heart. My second commitment is to be brave.

So when the spark came back, and I felt the thrill of fresh ideas, I was relieved and ecstatic. This was a whole new game. Listening to my soul first. Putting my heart ahead of what anyone else thought. Trusting in my creative intuition.

I can barely contain what a RUSH that was. And how profoundly liberating.

Which is exactly why I want that liberation and sovereignty for YOU.

So if I am coming out of a creative drought or a stressful time — I give myself permission to revel in the Kindle phase longer than I would if I felt energized and that my well was full. I'd bet that I experience short creative droughts a few times a year.

I choose to think of those droughts as fallow time. Like the fields and soil, I am far more productive when I have rest phases. Times to put down any expectations that I will be actively creating.

Other creatives rely on their creative endeavours to keep their mental health positive. To those friends, I always recommend finding something creative to do that doesn't equate to their work or passion or livelihood. Or working on their main project, but dialling back the time to a minimum so they can rest while still feeling the boost of making progress.

One perk of rest is that it gives you permission to have days when ideas just aren't showing up. Even the most prolific creatives need to play and rest. It reminds me that my creativity is safe. It's just taking a nap.

Ever since questioning if I was still a writer, there's a corner of my fearful mind that worries — If I step away for too long, will I lose the desire altogether? Will the spark go out?

The answer is — NO. The spark won't go out. That sweet spark is an intimate part of YOU.

The surprise perk of rest is feeling the creative spark come back. Oh my word! It's like drinking a big glass of water after a long run. Or re-discovering how amazing food tastes after a fast. You can hardly believe how *amazing* it feels to create again.

It's like coming back from a trip and revelling in how amazing your bed feels and how sweet your routines are. (Those same routines that drove you *bonkers* before you left!)

It's easy to take our creative projects for granted. When we work with them every day, they can get boring and frustrating. We might begin to resent them. So that break? It's best for everyone.

Much like the famous saying, "Absence makes the heart grow fonder." That timeless truth applies to your creativity, too.

When you return to it and it returns to you in the Kindle phase? You'll throw your arms around that creative spark with glee.

And dance with the heavens, knowing just how lucky you are.

***

Once you decide on one or two sparks to kindle, then what?

Since kindling a spark is a flirtation, not a commitment, I stay in a playful mode.

In the past, I pushed a project to get serious too fast. Purely to avoid the discomfort of not having a committed project. Thinking that being serious was more important than play. That the definition of being a professional was *always* having a big project on the books.

Do any of these sound familiar as haunting fears:

~ What if I never write/create again?

~ What if I'm burnt out and will never dream like before?

~ Who am I if I'm not writing/building a business?

~ What if my fellow writers find out I'm taking a break?

When you take care of yourself and your creativity, you *always* find a new project to care about. That is divine truth. You are designed to create. You are made for connecting.

Whether you're honouring your ancestors by carrying on their work or innovating the next, cutting-edge technology, you are 100% made to be creative. No matter how many bumps, scrapes, falls, or droughts you experience. Your creative inspiration will *always* find you.

***

Let's explore ways to play with your spark!

When I'm cultivating my spark, I use a lot of approaches. They all light me up — and can swap them in or out based on the feel of this project. I'm not prescriptive about what fuel to put on your fire.

Instead, I recommend listening closely to what nudges you forward. What piques your interest and sparks your excitement? The trick is to pay attention.

When I am playing with a book idea, I ask whether I need to play with developing the content (setting, characters, tone) or check out my niche (genre, sub-genre, writing style). Either path is a great way to get a sense of how interested you are. It can also shape how you move forward with writing the book.

I ask and feel into each activity. I'll get a sense of which one is "light and exciting" and which one feels "heavy and dull." I follow the approach that has excited energy. I trust it will light me up and the work goes much faster.

If I'm playing with the idea for a book and the exploration brings more questions, I know I'm onto something. Forward momentum is the Kindle effect. Your fuel is catching fire. If I'm exploring an idea for a course, I check in to ask how I'll feel teaching it. If it feels dull, I might set it aside. If I check in later and it still feels heavy or dull, then I know that's not the right course.

I've had sparks grow into webinars and guides and a lot of social media content. The whole time I was sharing, I also had a nagging feeling. Like something wasn't quite right. I started by teaching women about the significance of moon cycles. And what I wanted to teach was how to create with your unique rhythm — including the power of the moon's cycles.

It turned out that I was teaching a topic destined to be a small part of a much bigger project. It was a single tool ~ not the whole toolkit. This is the evolution that comes with kindling an idea ... and staying open to what it's ultimately meant to be.

For you, kindling might mean being out in the world. Listening to people. Jotting down ideas in a journal. Travelling to the location where you're setting a story. Or going to a seminar that's like what you're imagining. You might need to know what's out there, or you might prefer to brainstorm in a vacuum and forget what anyone else is doing.

You might listen to podcasts, dive down a YouTube rabbit hole, or read twenty books. You could hang out in communities that inspire you or find out the needs of who you're serving. You might create imagination boards on Pinterest. Some writers create Pinterest boards for how their characters look and dress, which actors will play the roles, what city the story is in, and make Spotify playlists that capture the story's mood.

Spontaneously follow where the idea takes you. Trust that the path with the momentum is how your heart guides you forward. And if you get stuck? Or feel bored? Go do something receptive. Take a walk. Meditate. Dance.

Let go for a little while and relax. Give the idea space. Let it come to you. Forcing the issue rarely works and is a direct path to unhappiness and (eventually) burnout. Kindling is a practice that trades pushing too hard for flowing with the creative dance. Knowing that if the idea is meant for you, you'll reconnect.

My trick during the Kindle phase is to balance receptive with active time. That gives me a push-pull effect. I make room to check in with how I'm feeling.

Some examples are:

~ Research using books or podcasts. Then go outside for a walk to allow for questions and connections.

~ Connect with a friend and share ideas. Then enjoy a silent drive home to let the sparks fly.

~ Dive deep into a topic on the web. Then pull out my journal to brainstorm.

~ Watch inspiring TV or films in my genre. Then make notes about what I love and what I don't.

Kindling the spark isn't necessarily about being productive and developing the project. I coach myself not to get caught up in deadlines or schedules. I'm testing out the relationship. I use this time to get a deeper sense of my interest.

Does my interest last beyond my first set of questions? Do I feel more (or less) of a connection? Does the research spark more curiosity? Or did I get swept up in someone else's enthusiasm when I picked this idea?

For sensitive creatives, that last one is tricky. It's easy to listen to someone else gush about their novel or talk or webinar and get caught up in the excitement. Just because they're excited doesn't mean the excitement will sustain for you. It's a classic case of FOMO (Fear Of Missing Out) or thinking someone else's path is yours.

There's no shame in it! Entire industries are built on FOMO. They count on the fact that you won't figure out that the whole thing feels like a jacket that never fit right. But because they're so convincing, you discount your intuition.

The flip side (another reason I keep my Kindle stage secret) is that you're excited, but when you tell your friend or sister about it, they dismiss it or make a face. Or your dad tells you that you'll never finish it because you've lost interest in everything else.

Or you're not convinced about the idea, but your colleague is convinced that it's a million dollar business and you have to take it all the way. That one's trickier because it feels so damn good!

Why wouldn't you want a friend or colleague to be wildly thrilled by what you're up to? The simple answer is — much like taking a date home to your family — *you're* not sure how you feel yet. The last thing you need is to get drunk on the acceptance you've been secretly craving. Trust me. The hangover *sucks*.

Your creative choices are going to lead you either to a detached no or a delighted commitment.

There is no loss in going down a path with ideas that you ultimately don't follow through on. You learn so much. And you get the relief of knowing that you aren't wasting your time! The longer I've been doing this, the faster I want to know if I'm *really* interested.

So, once you've had a heap of fun? Trust that you'll know the moment when juggling multiple ideas feels like juggling multiple romantic interests.

You might spend a lot of time evaluating and comparing and wondering and imagining. And the sooner you get a sense of the one that connects with your heart? The sooner you pour *all* that creative juice into the commitment you want to explore with depth.

Time is a precious resource that deserves to be spent wisely. So, I take time to play and explore. Enjoying the delight those qualities give me. While discovering more about the project. It's a wonderful time, and one that I treasure.

And as soon as I know if it's not for me? I bless it and send it back to the Divine for someone else to enjoy.

When I have a sense that I am excited about a project, that's when the butterflies arrive. The electric combination of nerves and anticipation. Especially if it's an arena that is new. Those challenge who I perceive myself to be and, even scarier, who others perceive me to be.

As creatives, this is often the biggest risk we take. I've confused people with the number of careers and businesses that I've had. What I do isn't something they understand. Or it scares them.

Counteract the fear or envy that others project onto you by surrounding yourself with bold creatives. People who take risks. Who have integrity. And hold your dreams with respect.

I thrive in the encouragement of these creative friends.

They know that it's a delicate balance between being bold and feeling vulnerable. I never want you to shut down your feelings. Feeling the risks will guide you to heal any blocks that held you back. You'll release any baggage you've picked up along the way.

Being a vibrant and authentic creative means feeling what it takes to leap into the arena. Shoving those feelings aside may work temporarily, but they will rear their head at some point.

Taking on creative projects that thrill you, that deepen your understanding of who you are, is a *huge* part of feeling alive.

Those projects light you up and draw your people to you. Why would I ever turn that down?

As Rumi says, "What you seek is seeking you."

The creative project that calls to your soul is meant to find you. And when it does, hold on tight.

Because the real adventure just started.

Chapter Ten

Creative Fire

O NE OF THE BEST feelings in the world is knowing you've found your next project. Whether it's a book, product, business, community, or collaboration, there is a moment when you *know* deep in your bones what's *next for you.*

Because no one else can choose that project. What's for you isn't for another. And vice versa. Even your creative bestie won't know if it's the right one. They rely on you to know. Then their job as your bestie is to wholeheartedly support what lights you up.

What does creative fire feel like? How do you know if *this* is the project to commit to?

You know in your gut and heart. Choosing a venture is a pulse of excitement, verging on obsession. It's the project that grabs you and wakes you at 4am. It's the book that you keep looking for — yet cannot find. It's the company you decide to start because you want to see that product in the world. It's the compulsion to offer what you needed when you started.

Creative fire doesn't need to consume you — but it will grab hold of your heart. As many projects as I've finished, there were hundreds that I *didn't* pursue.

Any big venture needs to be something that I truly care about. It's the idea that follows me on my walks and taunts me in the gym and pops in my head when I'm reading and whispers in my ear in the bookstore.

When I think about diving in, I feel a combination of anticipation and anxiety. I have few illusions anymore about the fortitude that's involved in completing a project. Even more if I plan to market it. And still, creating is such a thrill for me. It's the pulse that drives my curiosity. It's the delight that comes with learning. It's the exquisite confidence that comes from tackling a challenge.

The combo of anticipation and anxiety? That's my soul sensing the change this journey will unleash in my life. Every project I committed to has changed me.

In the film biz, each screenplay taught me what stories mattered to me, while teaching me about the craft. Some taught me how to relate to characters, some taught me the challenge of capturing an emotional journey, others taught me about researching a place that is notoriously secretive.

My novels taught me I was *absolutely* capable of writing a book. The first one taught me to trust myself and be brave. The second one taught me to be determined. The third one taught me how incredibly complicated it is to write a book that concludes a trilogy. And my lovely book, Blue Moon, taught me that trusting my personal timeline over a deadline really matters.

With every story, I learned from my protagonist's journey. I deepened my love for human beings and their courage. I discovered greater empathy for my villains (and the villains in my life). Each project guided me through at least one lesson. Or more likely seventeen lessons.

I've also created multiple businesses. One taught me to claim publicly what I love (and who cares what other people think!). Another taught me that CEOs can look and feel like me (when I didn't grow up with those role models).

I am deeply proud of each one, regardless of whether they were a worldly success. They're part of my journey. They're woven into the fabric of my being. And they were destined to be created by me.

A project that matters to you will *always* change you. That's a big part of why we do it.

Creating, for me, is a drive. An exploration. And a joy. It comes with challenges, delights, and fears. They course through me as I climb a new mountain, having only a tiny idea of how to reach the summit. But as anyone who loves adventure will tell you, that's what makes it fun!

If I am daring bravely as I create, I feel completely alive.

When I first started writing screenplays, I felt my soul directing my choices. Choosing the film industry and imagining that I could make a living writing stories were crucial steps. There was some compelling yet mysterious reason for me to pursue this path. I didn't know fully what it was, but I felt the pull on my heart and the excitement in my blood.

In hindsight, I see reasons why this was a crucial leap. I was raised in an artistic family, but one that firmly believed that art was a hobby. It was not a safe and secure place to make money. Art might make your heart happy, but it most certainly was not going to put a roof over your head and food in the fridge.

I watched as both of my parents had creative dreams that lit them up, only to shove them aside. I felt their regrets and their heartache. I'm not sure that they were meant to focus on their art or make it a career. But the rejection of believing in their talent left a heavy weight on their hearts.

For as long as I can remember, stories and my imagination were magnetic to me. I made up stories about strangers. I lived inside books and dreamt of a life far away from the hard reality that I lived as a child. Imagination was my best friend. Stories gave me hope and filled my mind with possibilities other than what I was living.

So when the film industry showed me a *career* as a creative writer, my mind was blown. No one had ever presented this as a career option. Or even a dream. And the indie publishing scene didn't exist yet. And very few authors made a lot of money publishing books.

I had zero desire to be a starving artist. I dreamt of being an artist who made millions, or at least thousands. So screenwriting seemed like a wild and magical possibility.

When I entered the film biz, my understanding of a thriving artist was one who made a lot of money and had their name in the credits on a movie. Over the years, I would discover that thriving involves much more than money and recognition. It means taking really good care of myself. Listening to my body. Trusting my intuition. And surrounding myself with kind people.

My soul took me to the film industry to revel in telling stories. To collaborate with others who believed in its transformative power as much as I did. And to show me that a whole industry existed where people made money through their creative gifts.

I *also* learned that being in a cycle of burnout made it *impossible* to feel which projects lit me up. Exhaustion left me confused and putting too much trust in other people's direction.

Some big soul lessons aren't pretty. They forge you in the crucible to come out with treasured wisdom. As hard as it was, I was deeply grateful to learn the value of trusting my guidance above anyone else's.

Once I understood that my inner wisdom was the guide to being a powerful creator *and* living a vibrant life? I'd stepped onto the yellow brick road of joyful creating.

***

The sign that my creative fire is blazing is when a project keeps nattering at me.

The idea (or character) nudges me, shows up on my walks, pushes its way into my thoughts when I am showering, pokes its way into my mind when I am working on my consulting gigs. I feel a little thrill when it whispers to me and piques my curiosity.

I feel a tug in my heart to dance with this story or business. I melt a little at the idea of spending time with it. Like a romance, I feel both relaxed and a little jumpy at the thought of committing. My eyes sparkle, my breath gets tight, and my hands shimmer.

These are all signs that the creative energy is building up. The persistent pull is strong and almost irresistible. I want to spend as much time as possible in the research, with the development, and in seeing this wonderful creation come to life.

I imagine it's the same nesting response that a pregnant mama experiences. I've never given birth to a human baby, but I have given birth to many screenplays, novels, and businesses. And from what my dear friends tell me, the feeling and stages are remarkably similar.

This is the point when I need to carve out regular time to be with my project. For some of you, this will be the hardest stage. It upends a lot of habits and unconscious patterns that create the rhythm of your life. When I haven't been writing consistently for a while, getting a rhythm back can feel a lot like working out after six months of being inactive.

And if you're a consistent writer who wants to start a product business or speak on podcasts every week?

The same holds true. Getting the rhythm is key - and being committed to your dream is important. The discomfort is real when you begin.

Even though I have been writing for many years, every time I start a new project, my mind goes bonkers. The possibility is exciting, and the risk feels petrifying. If you feel this, *great*! I mean it.

Those feelings mean you have found the project that *matters to you*. Never underestimate the importance of caring. That is the fuel for your fire. Caring means this creation will change you, light you up, and keep you going when you hit the steepest parts of the mountain.

When I approach a new project, my mind goes wild with questions and doubts. It sounds a little like this:

~ Am I doing this right?

~ Why does this book feel different?

~ What if this isn't the "one"?

~ This is going too fast /slow.

~ No one else feels this when they're starting.

~ I have no idea what I'm doing.

Every writer, creative, and entrepreneur feels this at the beginning. The biggest challenge in accelerating the creative fire is to move past the nerves that come with starting fresh.

In the creating process, we all have a stage that we love the most. Where we feel most in the groove. And we excel at it!

For me, it's the beginning stage. I understand that the initial weeks (and months) are going to feel awkward and a bit nerve-wracking. They also feel thrilling and fresh. The sheer adrenalin of the idea can fuel a lot of movement.

For others, the initial stage is terrifying and leads to freezing when facing a blank page or a fresh audience. If you tend towards procrastination, that habit can show up in spades when you're unsure how to get started. You'll find absolutely *anything* else to complete (including rearranging the contents of all your cupboards!) if you aren't sure how to handle the nervous feelings at the beginning.

For me, the middle gets challenging, and the tail end can be hella hard. I often feel like I am out of gas and just want to jump to a new fire. Or go travelling for a month.

Some people struggle in the middle because it can be like wandering in the desert. Like you've lost sight of why you started. While others push through the messy middle and *love* the exhilarating feeling of crossing the finish line. When they see the end, they accelerate speed.

No matter which stage you find thrilling and which one is nerve-wracking, the solution is to have support. That's how you cultivate the creative fire, keep it burning, and know you'll keep it going through to the end.

Support can look like a lot of things. An accountability buddy on your phone. A group that you meet with. A mentor or coach who guides you through the process. A friend who talks you through the bumps on the journey and cheers you on to the next step. Solid habits that keep you focused and committed and are the basis for your accountability.

You can sign up for programmes or courses that walk you through writing your book or creating your marketing plan with structure and deliverables. You could go to a writer's retreat where the expectation is to leave with an outline or draft. Or like Brené Brown (author of *Daring Greatly*), you could create your own retreat with trusted friends, great food, and discussing what you want, then capturing the ideas and content.

Support is a key element in countering the inevitable bumps that come with creating. This process is *designed* to challenge us. Because in challenge there is growth. In challenge we discover what we're made of. In challenge there is a deeper call to your soul.

We take on these projects to excavate our fears and move through them. The creative mythos that I grew up with was all about individual achievement. The solitary (and usually addicted) genius toiling away on his (yes, his) own while eschewing any help or financial support.

So many have debunked that myth. Yet, in our culture, the belief that struggling alone makes an achievement more valid is still pervasive. The struggle is not necessary.

You can choose to be solitary, but you never, *ever* have to walk the path alone.

Creating is a conversation between us and the Divine. This is the soul work inherent in creative projects.

That soul journey is a choice and is deeply connected to the courage that it takes to create what calls to you (and not to anyone else). That soul work includes having people who cheer you on and who want you to succeed.

During every creative endeavour, I bump up against my limitations. I find myself overthinking or facing down imposter syndrome. And while there are many times I talk myself back to work, there are also many times that I need the gentle encouragement of my team and collaborators.

Some days, it's as simple as knowing my editor is waiting for my draft. She whispers rallying words into my Instagram DMs and I feel my heart lifted. That little nudge, that kind boost of excitement, is enough to get the creative engine firing. To know that I am not just writing this book for me (though that is always where I start). But also having someone excited to read it.

While you don't need your full support plan in place before you start, I encourage you to have one. To think about what will prompt you, pull you, provoke you when you're struggling to move forward. Sometimes, this stuck place looks and feels like anxiety. And other times it will be procrastination, distraction, or just plain giving up.

These corners are incredibly tough to get out of once you're in them. That's why I want you to have a plan. To know at least two to three ways that you will have support throughout the journey. For me, the ideal choice is to have a group or a few friends who are on a parallel path.

I have my *Magic Mondays* group that meets to connect then write together for a few hours. When I was in the film biz, I had a monthly screenwriters' group that gave feedback and brainstormed on each other's projects. As an entrepreneur, I have one or two friends who have committed to being part cheerleader, part accountability partner.

If you are new in your creative endeavour or it feels especially scary, I recommend having a dedicated resource like a coach or a programme. That way, you're carried along and have the momentum of a group and deadlines (or milestones).

In my various careers, I've had a lot of folks reflect that I have incredible self-discipline. Some of that is inherent, and much of it comes from years of being responsible for my deadlines. Even with inner dedication, I've learned that I have *a lot* more fun on the journey when I include others. They also keep me creating consistently and at a quicker pace.

I love being able to relay where I am and what I've accomplished. Bragging to one another about the little things (that are actually big things) because you both understand what it takes to unravel a story conundrum or deliver the product labels you've been agonising over.

The delight of having company as you're creating is a big part of cultivating joy while creating. Sharing along the winding path of your journey makes *all* the difference in how you feel about your project. And ultimately, the energy that it conveys.

Imagine that the person who will eat the meals you're making or read the words you're writing will also be invited into the warm magic that you cultivated while creating. What a beautiful extension of the delight you created while forging your own brave path.

Why serve up an energy of struggle and frustration when you can offer your audience a scrumptious experience of delight? As you stoke and tend your own creative fire, you're imbuing your work with that love and joy. Your words will radiate the feeling that you want to convey. Uplifting your readers in their heart, mind, and soul.

***

The next commitment to make as you bravely plunge forth is pacing yourself. Any creative project worth the dedication and love in your heart requires time and a lot of energy. And that means remembering that the whole process is a marathon, not a sprint.

I remind myself of that truth *every* time. I can easily fire up and go, only to find myself halfway through a project wanting to throw the whole thing off a cliff. Which is incredibly demoralising. And if I give in to that pattern enough times? It becomes a self-defeating habit.

So, as you jump in, assume that it may take longer than you think. And you'll need to care for your energy to make it the whole way. Create a plan, even a simple one, of how much time you're committing.

I like to get a sense of how long I believe the project will take. Then I break that down into a weekly rhythm. It's easier for me to know how to fit weekly commitments into my life.

If I know what's involved, I can create a pretty accurate deadline. If I don't know what's involved, the deadline and deliverables may need to change. Regardless, make a plan. Commit to your deadlines. And if required, adjust them. Remember that the most important person you are delivering to (above your publisher, company, business partner, and community) is YOU.

Broken promises are most devastating to your heart. When you make a soul promise, keep it. Even if the timing needs to change (because ... life). Adjust your commitment. And keep it.

A key part of keeping my soul promises is prioritising my heart project ahead of other work. I juggle a lot of commitments, so it's easy to shove aside what matters to me to fulfil my other promises. Especially since I was raised to put others first.

Training myself to schedule my project *first* has been a lifelong undertaking. Learning along the way and forgiving myself (while recommitting) when I fumble that ball. If what you are creating is essential to your joy and satisfaction, I implore you to figure out how to put it first. If that means getting up early or staying up late, I trust that you can do that while also ensuring you get enough sleep, sunlight, and play.

Prioritising your soul work is both a privilege and a necessity. If I go too long without a project that nourishes my heart, I decline into cynicism and sometimes, despair. The world can be a lot for a sensitive, creative soul. Having an outlet for my expression (and energy) is the deal that I struck for having so much creative power at my fingertips.

That means I need to use it!

When I do, that fire warms and delights me. When I don't, I often discover how the same energy that gives life (creating) turns destructive. If you ever wondered why so many talented creatives implode with addiction or other sabotaging behaviour, it's because creative power is a force unto itself. And it needs a healthy, life-giving outlet.

If you don't tend your creative fire, it has the power to burn your whole house down. As a creative, you are made to wield fire. You must wield it with awareness and savvy habits.

Expression and untold stories eat us up from the inside. So while you need rest, inspiration, and replenishment, you equally need to respect your need to create. Are they all viable ideas? Heck no! I have written articles, launched YouTube channels, and attempted entire businesses that did not take flight or find an audience.

And still, I am proud of every attempt and every experiment. Each one gave me joy and helped me get clear on what really mattered to me enough to go the distance.

Once that fire is roaring, you need tools for creative momentum. As Rachel Hollis shared on her podcast, motivation is easy when you're excited. To finish the goal, you need momentum. That is the real magic. I have several go-tos for tending the fire, a.k.a. creative momentum.

The first is *community*. Find your creative friends - whether they are in person, online, or even in a book. Books like this one or encouraging reads like, "Big Magic," "The War of Art," "Keep Going," and "The Artist's Way." Books are wonderful companions and cheerleaders when the in-real-life version is too far away or you're just cultivating those relationships.

Community is everything from a friend or two who understand what you are doing to a group that you meet with regularly. By doing this, you're surrounding yourself with people who "speak your language."

There is a unique and kinda kooky experience to writing a novel, or being an actor, or designing large-scale landscapes, or launching an online business.

Friends and family may smile and nod and even say congratulations. Which is all wonderful. But it won't sustain you or keep your momentum when you're scared or tired and about to throw in the towel. You need folks who *get it*.

You need people who will say, "I really get it. I've been there. What do you need? How can I help?" Or maybe they will say, "I can feel how much you care about this. I think you might be scared. What's making you nervous?"

I can barely express how much it means when another author says, "Holy crap, I just went through that last week." Or "I had to drag myself to my desk this morning. I got you."

Even better, when you triumph and they dance around their living room and whoop like a wild woman! You know that they *really* understand what it took for you to accomplish your milestone.

Community is different from a coach or mentor or best friend. Community is made up of folks who are in your field or similar enough that you can turn to them when you're struggling and need a heartfelt boost. Community is the collection of people who really get you and can offer their experience or encouragement to keep you going.

My second go-to is *creating milestones* and, as a powerful bonus, getting an *accountability buddy*. On any creative journey, milestones are essential. Even if you're writing a magazine piece and you think putting some words on a page is all that's involved, you'll discover that's not true.

Any project that matters to you, and most definitely any project that needs more than one month, requires milestones. The key to momentum on longer projects is breaking them into manageable, smaller, and easily celebrated achievements.

That last one — easily celebrated — has been a game changer for me. The longer you're creating, the more you discover that patting yourself and others on the back is essential. You need little wins along the way. And they won't feel little. They will feel huge.

Loving every step makes all the difference in your joy meter and your persistence. Without celebrating the little moments, I have found myself in a rut. Convinced that I'll never make it to the finish line. And questioning why I even started.

Having a cheer squad who happy dance when you achieve your latest milestone is a lot like the amazing people who cheer on marathoners. Getting to mile 26 can look utterly impossible when you've just run 13 miles. I never would have made it past mile 14 if it weren't for the enthusiastic supporters on the sidelines. And the same might be true of me ever finishing a novel without my writing besties.

When I am writing and I reach another 10,000 word marker (as in 20,000 then 30,000), I breathe a sigh of relief. Each hurdle is like running its own race. A feat that deserves recognition and celebration! And when I finish a significant draft? I buy something personal that will forever remind me of my accomplishment.

Writing the third book in my *Great Lands* series was harder than writing all three of my other books combined. I had never written the final book in a series. I hadn't thought about all the plot and character threads that needed to be woven together to have the ending be satisfying. Completing that book felt a little like my creative Ironman race.

So when I finished, I purchased a Pyhrra necklace. One with a sweet compass that symbolises being connected and oriented to my heart's path. Every time I wear that necklace, I think about its origin story. I remember that I bought it to celebrate a big triumph.

That triumph included many little milestones along the way. I leaned on my accountability allies to achieve it. Whether you share what you're up to with your email list or a friend, make sure that you declare your project and when you hope to finish.

You don't have to give details (especially if you're keeping all that wonderful creative magic to pour into your creation). But you can leverage making your project public

— so you keep going. You could even make your readers your cheer squad! I know writers who do exactly that.

While writing *Queen*, I had my writer friends, my Instagram followers, my mother- and sister-in-law, my editor, and others all asking how it was going. This can feel stressful if you're not showing up for your commitment. But I like knowing that people are nudging me to complete the creative projects that really matter to my heart.

My third go-to is to *choose your ideal time* to create and protect it like a lioness. The easiest thing in the world is to shrug off our creative time when your life is full of commitments. Jobs, children, pets, partners, homes, family, appointments. They take up a lot of space in your head and pull at the strings of your heart.

I've been doing this for two decades, and I still need to be firm about my creative time. The world I was raised in did not prize creative projects, nor did it reward me for putting my desires first. Quite the contrary. I still have voices in my head that call it selfish, foolish, and a waste of time.

Those voices are precisely why I need to listen to my heart, not my head.

Every time I finish 15 minutes or two hours of soulful creative work, I beam with satisfaction and delight. I have to shoo away dozens of mental demons to sit down, but when I do? I come away shining light like a thousand stars.

You will feel this, too. That you've honoured your soul. Your calling. Your passion.

So, make it your mission to find out what time works for you. Like working out, I need to create in the morning or it won't happen. Can I create at night? Yes. Have I created at night? Yes. But it also takes ten times the effort for me to do it. And it typically only happens if I have an imminent deadline.

Once I have momentum, it becomes easier and easier to show up. If this habit is new for you, combining it with your accountability ally might be a great way to reinforce the commitment. This will show them (and you!) that you're making progress.

And remember that your creative rhythm is yours to determine. Whether you create seven days a week or three days a week, choose your flow and commit to it. Your flow doesn't have to look like anyone else's. It just needs to honour *you*.

The greatest skill that you develop as a creative and entrepreneur is setting deadlines and completing them. Do they change? *For sure.* So never let developing "the perfect plan" get in the way of starting. The plan will change.

Knowing that every plan changes once you're on the creative road is liberating. If you have a skeleton of an idea of your timeline and your key milestones, you're ready.

The more you respect your goals and milestones, the more you respect your gifts and talents. Your inspiration and momentum will grow through that respect.

And remember ~ your creative fire warms you and touches others.

To stoke that fire is not a selfish act. The more you take care of your creativity, the brighter you shine. People will gather close to be warmed by your dedication. They will feel your faith and be inspired to start their projects.

This is the beauty and the gift of the creative collective. We fuel ourselves and one another when we're true to our souls. We uplift each other as we walk our paths. And we rejuvenate each other with our joy, delight, and power.

The fire in your heart is one spark in a universal bonfire. Let's light it up together.

Chapter Eleven

The Gift

B EING CREATIVE IS THE joy of my life.

And like in any relationship, there are ebbs and flows. Hard times and sweet times. Challenges and gifts. When I approach each challenge with love and commitment, intimacy deepens.

If you've received anything from this book, I hope you found compassion for your heart and curiosity for your process. Joyfully creating is a journey to intimacy with your desires and expression.

It's a creative lifestyle that embraces your humanness and celebrates your divinity.

There will inevitably be times when you feel less creative. Less vibrant. And need to receive instead of give. In the past, this has been when little mental gremlins pop into my mind and cause all kinds of havoc. Torturing me and stirring up feelings of "doing it wrong."

Any notion of being or getting it wrong is a sure-fire symptom of perfectionism. And the fastest way to douse your self-compassion and creative flame.

When I've drifted into seasons of creative winter, it's been hard to endure. Until I realized that our creativity goes through seasons. Just like mother nature.

My wish for all of us is to understand that a day, week, or months of creative winter is not a sign to panic. It's actually a sign to pull in, dress cosy, make a mug (or seven) of hot chocolate and tend to that inner fire.

There's a reason our ancestors had festive days during the darkest time of winter. To spark our imagination. To kindle hope in our hearts. To remind us that the sun would rise again.

The longer I create, the more I revere and trust the process. I believe that this drive and desire to create is my Divine essence. Listening to it and tending it is a gift. This is the path that I chose. Every day is an opportunity to learn and grow to understand my path.

Your creative path is meant to be different from mine, your partner's, your family's and every other being on earth. What we have in common is the need to take care of that path. To remember that we choose to be here and grow from what it has to teach us.

As we come to the end of our time together, I wonder what these words have inspired in you. What got rattled?

Did you resist the idea of taking better care of yourself? Or are you lit up by the notion of creativity being a rhythm like the ocean? That there is an inflow and an outflow.

I hope this book raised many questions. That it sparked your curiosity. That you rejected some ideas and wholeheartedly adopted others.

As a creative community, we have much to learn and explore together. The thrill for me is understanding that every day holds the mystery and magic of discovery.

My next project may take me on a wild ride that gallops at the speed of a thousand horses. While this one has been a steady heartbeat, moving at the pace of a gentle summer tide.

More than anything, I want the creatives of this world to understand what a gift we are. To love the talents that burst inside us. To adore the crazy ride that we choose every day. To surround ourselves with people who understand how deeply we treasure what we do. Even on the days that we want to throw our manuscripts out the window.

When you remember the gift, you remember every step is magic.

Every experience is a treasure. Every feeling has a lesson. And every person brings you growth. My greatest delights come from the stories I've told, the people I've loved, and the adventures I've taken. These are my lifeblood. My vitality.

And I want to keep taking bolder risks in each of those areas of my life.

What does your creativity give you? Have you loved every moment, no matter how hard? Have you cursed it or blessed it? How do you want it to make you feel?

You deserve to love every moment and savour every experience. You are a fire and a treasure. You are a magical being who brings forth novels, businesses, products, communities, and ideas.

Is there really anything better than that?

Joyful creating is the deep belief and the habits that centre you. They support you to create from a spirit of delight. That doesn't mean every day will be sunshine and rainbows. You will have days filled with thunderstorms and hail.

Now you know that when winter arrives, you bundle up and double-down. You tend to your creative heart. And you throw away old notions of hiding in isolation, resenting other artists, or believing that the spark will never return.

You're well-versed in calling out the old lies, so you can make wide open space for the truth of your innate power. The fire that will burn inside you until the day you take your final breath.

And so, to wrap our time together, I encourage you to ask what you dream of creating. What do you wish to leave behind? What project would thrill you? What risk would light you up?

Most of all, what makes you come alive and want to dive in head-first? That is the power of true and vital creativity. The essence of who you are and what you came to be.

Now, if you'll excuse me, I have some shenanigans to start.

Much love, Kate

P.S. The sister book of this one is called *Joyful Making: How to Stop Overthinking and Start Making Magic.* It's brimming with rituals and habits to build your joyful creative practice. If you want to know more, subscribe at www.katetremills.com/joinus.

Gratitudes

Books are woven from words and community. I'm grateful for the support of these lovely people.

Wonderful Editor
Friel Black – for being a talented and wise editor who guided me between drafts.

First Readers
Martha, Jill, and Sheila - for catching the typos, tangents, and opportunities.

Encouraging Friends
Allison, Mei Ling, and Michelle – for showing up and being generous when I needed a pep talk.

Substack Supporters
For being proof that my words didn't vanish into the ether and can uplift people around the world.

Loving Family
Kevin - for listening and encouraging me to be brave.

Author's Note

Hey there, creative soul!

Thank you so much for reading *Joyful Creating*. Writing this book was a delight that reminded me how much I've gained from making things — stories, businesses, and bold ideas. The fact that you're here, on this final page, means the world to me.

If this book kindled something in you — a breath of inspiration, a sense of possibility, or a good laugh on a grumbly day — I'd be grateful if you'd consider leaving a review on Amazon. Reviews help other readers discover the book. And your words truly make a difference.

If you think someone in your life would love this book? Please share it with them. Word of mouth from fellow creatives is pure magic!

With a grateful heart,
Kate

About the Author

Kate Tremills is a writer, speaker, and myth-loving creative who ditched the film biz to chase fate and dragons in her fantasy novels. With two novel series and a flair for mischief, she stirs up magic on Substack. She writes regularly about her creative journey. Kate offers courses teaching others to ditch the grind and create projects that light them up. She lives on Vancouver Island, riding sea breezes and dubious amounts of coffee.

Substack | Instagram | Website | Amazon |

Joyful Making

How to stop overthinking & start making magic

If Joyful Creating rekindled your spark, Joyful Making keeps it glowing—right to the finish line.

Your creative companion for doing without losing yourself to the grind. Instead of forcing your work, you'll build a steady, joy-filled practice that strengthens your confidence and helps you complete what matters most.

With nine soulful principles, Kate offers insight and habits to build your momentum. Whether you're writing a novel, starting a business, or shaping a personal project.

Joyful Making is your invitation to create with clarity, heart, and magic.

Coming Soon in Spring 2026

Messenger

They burned her world to the ground. Now she must rise from the ashes to stop the shadow consuming it.

As darkness sweeps the Great Lands, Gabriella's warnings fall on deaf ears. Her father, the king, refuses to see the storm coming—until the Great Prince arrives. Armies are shattered, her sister stolen, and Gabriella is forced into hiding.

Years later, a mysterious figure cloaked in ancient magic finds her and sees her as the messenger fated to defy the Prince. Guided by his wisdom and her awakening gift of prescience, Gabriella sets out on a perilous journey.

As she faces ruthless enemies and impossible odds, Gabriella uncover a fierce, untamed magic —and the strength to reclaim a broken world.

Buy Messenger on Amazon

Blue Moon

Some jobs change your life. This one rewrites fate and ignites an ancient grudge.

Helen wasn't looking for a new job—or to crash a feud centuries in the making. When she follows a pull into Logan & Associates, she finds more than antique furniture and ominous silence. She finds Logan—a man she's never met, who knows her name, her past, and maybe even her future.

Elsewhere, the Three Sisters of Fate are making ... adjustments. For reasons they'd rather not explain, their hopes ride on a woman with potent intuition and no filter.

An enemy is rising who feeds on chaos and sees Helen as the barrier to his plans. What started as a whim is about to reshape more than one future.

Buy Blue Moon on Amazon

More Books

THE GREAT LANDS
Messenger
Warrior
Queen

FATED
Blue Moon
Assembly of the Gods

www.ingramcontent.com/pod-product-compliance
Lightning Source LLC
Chambersburg PA
CBHW020423150626
46554CB00014B/2467